JN358094

영어회화 3단계 집중 훈련

팟캐스트
영어
스터디

라이언 강, 마이클 사이먼 지음

바이링구얼

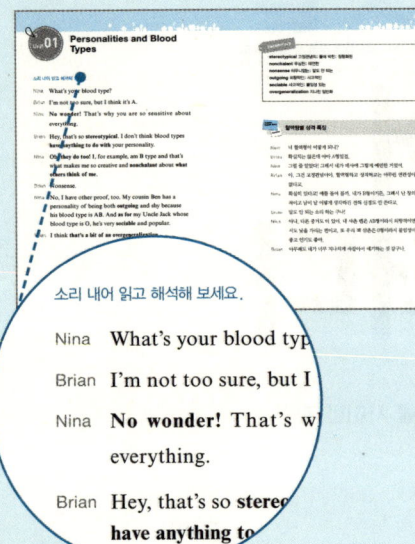

오늘의 주제와 본문
일상에서 자주 다루는 주제의 에세이 또는 대화문으로 네이티브 표현과 뉘앙스 익히기

토론 내용
스터디 하는 사람들과 서로 질문하며 영어로 토론하기

핵심 표현 활용하기
본문의 핵심 표현에 관해 더 자세히 알아보고 활용법 익히기

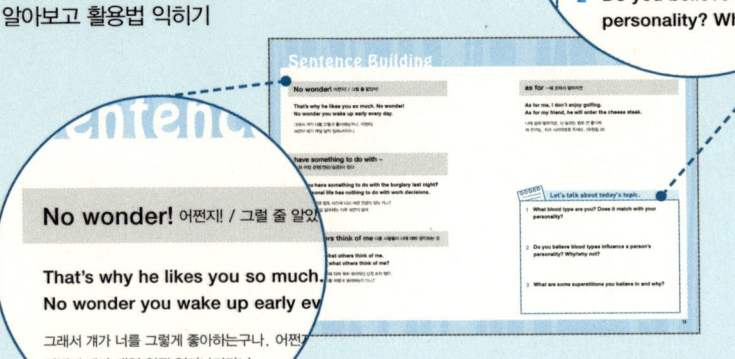

연습 문제

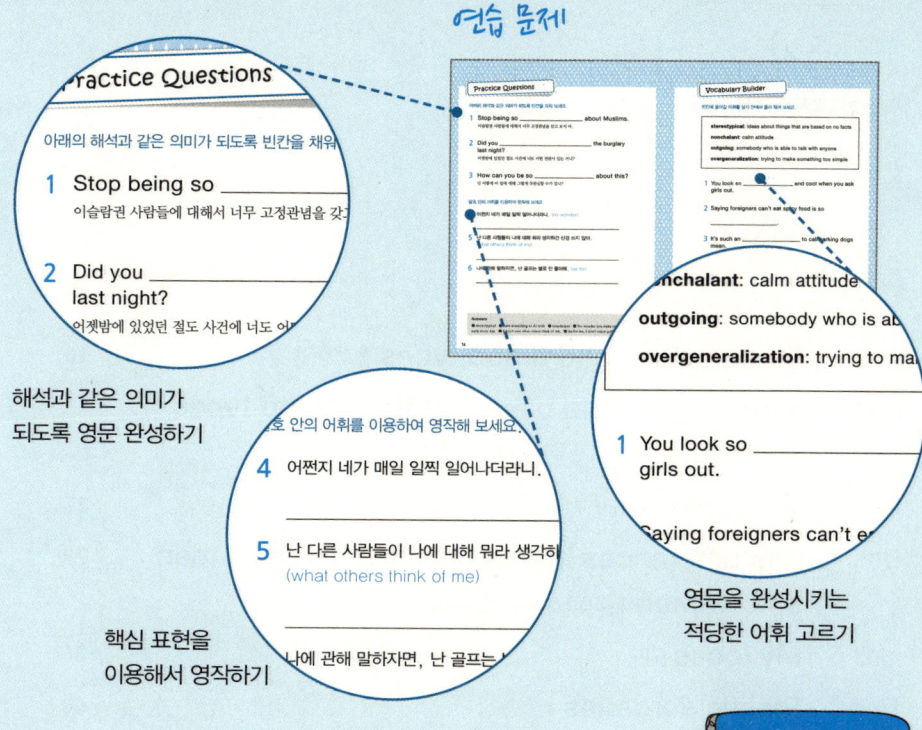

해석과 같은 의미가
되도록 영문 완성하기

핵심 표현을
이용해서 영작하기

영문을 완성시키는
적당한 어휘 고르기

학습 방법

1 팟캐스트 강의 듣기
  ❶ 책을 보며 팟캐스트 강의를 듣고 공부하기
  ❷ 각 유닛의 연습문제 Practice Questions와 Vocabulary Builder 풀기.

2 섀도잉과 녹음 과제
  ❶ 본문 mp3파일을 들으며 동시에 따라 말하는 섀도잉 훈련하기. 성우의 발음과 억양을 최대한 가깝게 흉내 내어 말하는 것이 핵심! 많이 연습할수록 좋다.
  ❷ 본문 지문을 읽으며 스마트폰으로 녹음하기. 성대모사를 한다고 생각하고 성우의 발음 및 억양을 최대한 비슷하게 말하기.

3 스터디 그룹 / 독학
  ❶ 한 사람씩 돌아가며 지문을 한 문장씩 읽고 해석하기. 대화문으로 이루어진 본문은 둘이서 역할극 해 보기.
  ❷ Today's topic에 관해 영어로 서로 질문하고 답하기

Part 1

Unit 1	**Personalities and blood types** 혈액형별 성격 특징	10
Unit 2	**Matching people based on their blood types** 혈액형 궁합	16
Unit 3	**My personality** 성격	22
Unit 4	**The differences in personalities between men and women** 남자와 여자의 성격 차이	28
Unit 5	**My looks** 외모	34
Unit 6	**Plastic surgeries** 성형수술	40
Unit 7	**Meeting people through online dating sites** 온라인 만남	46
Unit 8	**Ever been in a relationship with a younger man/an older woman?** 연하남/연상녀와 사귄 적이 있나요?	52
Unit 9	**Ever been in a relationship with a player?** 바람둥이와 사귄 적이 있나요?	58
Unit 10	**Who pays when on a date?** 데이트 비용은 누가 내나요?	64

Part 2

Unit 11	**Embarrassing drunk nights** 술자리 실수 경험	72

Unit 12 **Memorable gifts** 기억에 남는 선물 … 78
Unit 13 **Dream wedding** 꿈의 결혼식 … 84
Unit 14 **Breakfast** 아침 식사 … 90
Unit 15 **Do you cook?** 요리하세요? … 96
Unit 16 **Grocery shopping** 장보기 … 102
Unit 17 **Food shows on TV** TV 먹방 … 108
Unit 18 **School uniforms** 교복 … 114
Unit 19 **Study groups** 스터디 모임 … 120
Unit 20 **Social clubs** 동호회 … 126

Part 3

Unit 21 **Do you share any chores around your house?** 집안일을 분담해서 하나요? … 134
Unit 22 **Noise between apartment floors** 층간 소음 … 140
Unit 23 **Sexual harassment** 성추행 … 146
Unit 24 **Online shopping** 온라인 쇼핑 … 152
Unit 25 **Buying directly from sites abroad** 해외 직구 … 158
Unit 26 **Do you have religion?** 종교가 있나요? … 164
Unit 27 **Podcasts** 팟캐스트 … 170
Unit 28 **Fitness craze** 몸짱 열풍 … 176
Unit 29 **Tattoos** 문신 … 182
Unit 30 **Fortune-telling** 점 … 188

Unit 1	**Personalities and blood types**
	혈액형별 성격 특징
Unit 2	**Matching people based on their blood types**
	혈액형 궁합
Unit 3	**My personality**
	자신의 성격
Unit 4	**The differences in personalities between men and women**
	남자와 여자의 성격 차이
Unit 5	**My looks**
	외모
Unit 6	**Plastic surgeries**
	성형수술
Unit 7	**Meeting people through online dating sites**
	온라인 만남
Unit 8	**Ever been in a relationship with a younger man/an older woman?**
	연하남/연상녀와 사귄 적이 있나요?
Unit 9	**Ever been in a relationship with a player?**
	바람둥이와 사귄 적이 있나요?
Unit 10	**Who pays when on a date?**
	데이트 비용은 누가 내나요?

Personalities and blood types

소리 내어 읽고 해석해 보세요.

Nina   What's your blood type?

Brian   I'm not too sure, but I think it's A.

Nina   **No wonder!** That's why you are so sensitive about everything.

Brian   Hey, that's so **stereotypical**. I don't think blood types **have anything to do with your personality**.

Nina   Oh, they do too! I, for example, am type B and that's what makes me so creative and **nonchalant** about **what others think of me**.

Brian   **Nonsense!**

Nina   No, I have other proof, too. My cousin Ben has a personality of being both **outgoing** and shy because his blood type is AB. And **as for** my Uncle Jack, whose blood type is O, is very sociable and popular.

Brian   I think that's a bit of an **overgeneralization**.

Vocabulary

No wonder! 어쩐지! / 그럴 줄 알았어!
stereotypical 고정관념의, 틀에 박힌, 정형화된
have something to do with ~ ~와 어떤 관련[연관/상관]이 있다
nonchalant 무심한, 태연한
what others think of me 다른 사람들이 나에 대해 생각하는 것
nonsense 터무니없는, 말도 안 되는
outgoing 외향적인, 사교적인
as for ~에 관해서 말하자면
overgeneralization 지나친 일반화

혈액형별 성격 특징

Nina   너 혈액형이 뭐야?

Brian   확실하진 않은데, 아마 A형일걸.

Nina   그럴 줄 알았어! 그래서 네가 매사에 그렇게 예민한 거였구나.

Brian   야, 그건 고정관념이야. 혈액형하고 성격은 아무런 상관이 없어.

Nina   확실히 있어! 예를 들어, 난 B형이라 창의적이고 남이 날 어떻게 생각하는지 전혀 신경 안 쓰거든.

Brian   말도 안 돼!

Nina   아냐, 다른 증거도 있어. 내 사촌 벤은 AB형이라서 외향적이면서도 낯을 가리는 편이야. 또 우리 잭 삼촌은 O형인데 붙임성이 좋고 인기도 많아.

Brian   아무래도 좀 지나치게 일반화시키는 것 같은데.

Sentence Building

No wonder! 어쩐지! / 그럴 줄 알았어!

That's why he likes you so much. No wonder!
No wonder you wake up early every day.

그래서 걔가 너를 그렇게 좋아하는구나. 어쩐지!
어쩐지 네가 매일 일찍 일어나더라니.

have something to do with ~
~와 어떤 관련[연관/상관]이 있다

Did you have something to do with the burglary last night?
My personal life has nothing to do with work decisions.

어젯밤에 있었던 절도 사건에 너도 어떤 연관이 있는 거니?
내 사생활은 직장 업무와는 아무 상관이 없어.

what others think of me 다른 사람들이 나에 대해 생각하는 것

I don't care what others think of me.
Do you know what others think of me?

난 다른 사람들이 나에 대해 뭐라 생각하건 신경 쓰지 않아.
넌 다른 사람들이 나를 어떻게 생각하는지 아니?

as for ~에 관해서 말하자면

As for me, I don't enjoy golfing.
As for my friend, he will order the cheese steak.

나에 관해 말하자면, 난 골프는 별로 안 좋아해.
제 친구는, 치즈 스테이크로 주세요. (주문할 때)

Let's talk about today's topic.

1. What blood type are you? Does it match with your personality?

2. Do you believe blood types influence a person's personality? Why/why not?

3. What are some superstitions you believe in and why?

Practice Questions

아래의 해석과 같은 의미가 되도록 빈칸을 채워 보세요.

1 Stop being so _____ about Muslims.
이슬람권 사람들에 대해서 너무 고정관념을 갖고 보지 마.

2 Did you _____ the burglary last night?
어젯밤에 있었던 절도 사건에 너도 어떤 연관이 있는 거니?

3 How can you be so _____ about this?
넌 어떻게 이 일에 대해 그렇게 무관심할 수가 있니?

괄호 안의 어휘를 이용하여 영작해 보세요.

4 어쩐지 네가 매일 일찍 일어나더라니. (no wonder)
_____

5 난 다른 사람들이 나에 대해 뭐라 생각하건 신경 쓰지 않아.
(what others think of me)
_____

6 나에 관해 말하자면, 난 골프는 별로 안 좋아해. (as for)
_____

Answers

❶ stereotypical ❷ have something to do with ❸ nonchalant ❹ No wonder you wake up early every day. ❺ I don't care what others think of me. ❻ As for me, I don't enjoy golfing.

Vocabulary Builder

빈칸에 들어갈 어휘를 상자 안에서 골라 적어 보세요.

> **stereotypical**: ideas about things that are based on no facts
>
> **nonchalant**: calm attitude
>
> **outgoing**: somebody who is able to talk with anyone
>
> **overgeneralization**: trying to make something too simple

1. You look so _____ and cool when you ask girls out.

2. Saying foreigners can't eat spicy food is so _____.

3. It's such an _____ to call barking dogs mean.

4. Bill is so cool! He's so _____.

Answers
❶ nonchalant ❷ stereotypical ❸ overgeneralization ❹ outgoing

Matching people based on their blood types

소리 내어 읽고 해석해 보세요.

I **went on a blind date** last night. The girl and I really **hit it off** until the moment she **brought up the subject** of blood types. **Apparently**, this girl believes that certain blood types are more **compatible** with each other **when it comes to** dating. I'm like, oh, really? She said that her blood type is A, so she can't stand guys whose blood type is B because they are all players and they only care about themselves. And she likes guys with blood type O or AB blood because they are fun to be with. Then, here comes the climax, when I told her my blood type was also A, she said she couldn't go out with me because both of us would be **timid** and **indecisive**. Well, I don't think she's my type either.

Vocabulary

go on a date 데이트를 하다
go on a blinde date 소개팅을 하다
hit it off (with) (~와) 죽이 맞다, 쿵짝이 맞다
bring up a[the] subject 화제를 꺼내다
apparently 듣자 하니, 보아하니, 분명히
compatible 호환이 되는, 화합할 수 있는
when it comes to ~에 있어서는, ~에 관한 한, ~할 때가 되면
timid 소심한
indecisive 우유부단한

혈액형 궁합

어젯밤에 소개팅을 했다. 소개팅녀와 난 정말 죽이 잘 맞았어, 그녀가 혈액형에 관한 얘기를 꺼내기 전까지 말이야. 딱 보아하니 그녀는 연애할 때 서로 더 잘 맞는 혈액형이 있다고 믿고 있더라고. 그래서 난, 에이, 정말요? 이랬지. 그녀가 말하길 자기는 A형이라서 B형 남자와는 상극이래. B형 남자들은 죄다 바람둥이에다가 자기밖에 모른다면서 말이야. O형이나 AB형 남자들은 같이 있으면 재밌어서 좋대. 그런데, 정말 가관인 건, 난 A형이라고 했더니 나하고는 사귈 수가 없다네. 이유인즉슨 우리 둘 다 소심한 데다가 우유부단할 거라나 뭐라나. 참 내, 그 여자도 내 타입은 아냐.

Sentence Building

go on a date 데이트를 하다

Do you want to go on a date with me?
Aaron and I went on a date last night and it was awesome.

나랑 데이트 할래?
애런하고 어젯밤에 데이트했는데 정말 좋았어.

hit it off ~와 죽이 맞다, 쿵짝이 맞다

Bonnie and I really hit it off last night.
Did you hit it off with your blind date?

보니하고 나하고 어젯밤에 정말 쿵짝이 잘 맞아서 재미있었어.
소개팅한 사람하고는 잘됐니?

bring up a[the] subject 화제를 꺼내다

I'm going to bring up the subject at our next meeting.
Why do you always have to bring up that subject while we're eating?

다음 회의 때 그 얘기를 꺼낼 거야.
넌 왜 꼭 먹을 때마다 그런 얘기를 꺼내야만 하는 거니?

when it comes to ~에 있어서는, ~에 관한 한, ~할 때가 되면

When it comes to cooking, I'm the best.
I can't focus when it comes to taking a test.

요리에 관한 한, 내가 최고야.
시험을 볼 때면 난 집중을 못하겠더라.

 **Let's talk about today's topic.**

1. Do you get nervous when you are on a blind date? What kind of things do you usually talk about on a blind date?

2. Do you believe that people with certain blood types are more compatible?

3. How do you feel about the people who firmly believe that blood types dictate personality traits?

Practice Questions

아래의 해석과 같은 의미가 되도록 빈칸을 채워 보세요.

1 What do you think of guys who are _____?
우유부단한 남자들에 대해 어떻게 생각하니?

2 She is very _____ but sweet.
그녀는 소심하긴 하지만 다정해.

3 Do you want to _____ with me?
나랑 데이트할래?

괄호 안의 어휘를 이용하여 영작해 보세요.

4 보니하고 나하고 어젯밤에 정말 쿵짝이 잘 맞아서 재미있었어. (hit it off)
_____

5 다음 회의 때 그 얘기를 꺼낼 거야. (bring up the subject)
_____

6 요리에 관한 한, 내가 최고야. (when it comes to)
_____

Answers
❶ indecisive ❷ timid ❸ go on a date ❹ Bonnie and I really hit it off last night.
❺ I'm going to bring up the subject at our next meeting. ❻ When it comes to cooking, I'm the best.

Vocabulary Builder

빈칸에 들어갈 어휘를 상자 안에서 골라 적어 보세요.

> **apparently**: when you understand something based on information
>
> **compatible**: possible to be, work, or play together
>
> **timid**: shy
>
> **indecisive**: unable or difficult to make choices

1 Don't be so _____! Talk to some people at the party.

2 Betty and I are so _____. It's like we can read each other's minds.

3 Stop being so _____ and just pick one already.

4 _____ we're going to Lotteworld next weekend.

Answers
❶ timid ❷ compatible ❸ indecisive ❹ Apparently

My personality

소리 내어 읽고 해석해 보세요.

Some people tell me I have a good personality. They say I'm **easy to talk to**. Well, I guess it's good that they think that way. But **the way I feel** is that I'm not **at ease** when I talk to people. That's probably because I care too much about what they think of me. Gosh, I'm so **self-conscious**. I know it's really hard to change my personality or maybe even impossible, but sometimes I just wish I wasn't the way I am now. How nice it would be if I were more **carefree**, **sensible**, reliable, thoughtful, and also funny! Am I **asking for too much**? I guess I am. Well, I am who I am. I don't have to change anything. At least, I'm not as **self-absorbed**, **obnoxious**, and **cranky** as some of my friends are. (I hope they don't read this, haha.)

Vocabulary

easy to talk to 대화하기 편한, 말이 잘 통하는
the way I feel 내 생각에는, 내가 느끼기에는
at ease 걱정 없이, 마음이 편안한
self-conscious 남의 시선을 의식하는
carefree 속 편한, 근심 걱정 없는
sensible 분별 있는, 지각 있는, 합리적인
ask for too much 원하는 것이 너무 많다, 무리한 요구를 하다
self-absorbed 자신에게만 몰두한, 자기밖에 모르는
obnoxious 아주 불쾌한, 몹시 기분 나쁜
cranky 짜증을 내는

성격

사람들이 나보고 성격이 좋다고 한다. 내가 대화하기 편한 상대라나. 음, 그렇게 생각해 준다니 뭐 나쁠 거야 없지. 그런데 내가 느끼기에 난 사람들과 대화할 때 별로 편하지가 않다. 아마 내가 너무 사람들의 눈치를 봐서 그런지도 모르겠다. 맙소사, 난 왜 이리 남의 시선을 의식하는 걸까. 물론 성격을 바꾼다는 게 쉬운 일도 아니고 어쩌면 불가능할 수도 있겠지만, 어떨 때는 정말 성격을 확 바꿀 수 있으면 좋겠다는 생각이 들 때가 있다. 느긋하고 분별력 있고 믿음직스럽고 사려 깊으면서 게다가 재미있기까지 한 그런 성격이면 얼마나 좋을까! 좀 무리인가? 좀 그런 듯. 암튼, 나는 나니까. 있는 그대로 살아야지. 그래도, 난 최소한 자기밖에 모르고 무례하고 짜증만 내는 그런 내 친구들 같지는 않으니까. (제발 그 친구들이 이 글을 읽지 않기를 바라며, 하하.)

Sentence Building

easy to talk to 대화하기 편한, 말이 잘 통하는

Bobby is just so easy to talk to. We talk for hours.
I like to think I'm easy to talk to.

바비는 말이 정말 잘 통해. 우리는 만나면 몇 시간씩 수다를 떨어.
난 내가 대화하기 편한 상대라고 믿고 싶어.

the way I feel 내 생각에는, 내가 느끼기에는

That's the way I feel and I hope you can understand that.
The way I feel is that these rules need to change.

내 생각은 그러니 네가 이해해 주길 바란다.
난 이 규정들이 바뀌어야 한다고 생각해.

at ease 걱정 없이, 마음이 편안한

Try to feel at ease when you are stressed.
When are you most at ease?

스트레스 받을 때는 편안한 마음을 가지도록 노력해 보세요.
가장 마음이 편할 때가 언제니?

ask for too much 원하는 것이 너무 많다, 무리한 요구를 하다

You're asking for too much.
I hope I'm not asking for too much when I say I love you.

넌 너무 무리한 요구를 하고 있어.
나의 사랑 고백이 너무 부담스럽게 느껴지진 않았으면 좋겠네요.

Let's talk about today's topic.

1 What do you think your main personality traits are?

2 What do you want to change about your personality?

3 What personality trait do you not want in a guy/girl?

Practice Questions

아래의 해석과 같은 의미가 되도록 빈칸을 채워 보세요.

1 I used to be very _____.
   난 예전에 남들의 시선을 많이 의식했었어.

2 Gwen was a lot more _____ than I thought.
   그웬은 내 생각보다 훨씬 더 자기밖에 모르는 여자였어.

3 David is so _____ I can't stand him.
   데이빗은 너무 무례해서 정말 더 이상은 못 봐주겠어.

괄호 안의 어휘를 이용하여 영작해 보세요.

4 바비는 말이 정말 잘 통해. (easy to talk to)
   _____

5 스트레스 받을 때는 편안한 마음을 가지도록 노력해 보세요. (at ease)
   _____

6 넌 너무 무리한 요구를 하고 있어. (ask for too much)
   _____

Answers

❶ self-conscious ❷ self-absorbed ❸ obnoxious ❹ Bobby is just so easy to talk to.
❺ Try to feel at ease when you are stressed. ❻ You are asking for too much.

Vocabulary Builder

빈칸에 들어갈 어휘를 상자 안에서 골라 적어 보세요.

> **sensible**: acting on good judgment and logical ideas
>
> **self-absorbed**: being only interested in yourself and what you do
>
> **thoughtful**: showing careful attitude especially towards other people
>
> **obnoxious**: very unpleasant and rude
>
> **cranky**: easily irritated or annoyed

1 You seem awfully _____ today. Did I do something wrong?

2 Sandra was so _____ with herself. She didn't notice the people around her.

3 Michael is the most _____ guy I've ever met in my life.

4 Trying to stay up all night for two days in a row is not a _____ thing to do.

5 How _____ of you!

Answers
❶ cranky ❷ self-absorbed ❸ obnoxious ❹ sensible ❺ thoughtful

The differences in personalities between men and women

소리 내어 읽고 해석해 보세요.

I like my girlfriend so much and I know that she likes me too. But sometimes I feel so **frustrated** when she tells me that I don't understand what she wants. How would I know what she wants if she doesn't tell me? She just **talks in circles**. And when she asks me for advice, I tell her exactly what to do. But she tells me that I'm too **straightforward**. And sometimes she wants to go shopping **with no intention of** buying anything. I think that's **such a waste of time**. I mean, why go shopping if you're not buying anything? I know that people say that women are emotional and **process-oriented** while men are **rational** and **goal-oriented** but still, this is too much for me.

Vocabulary

frustrated 좌절감을 느끼는, 불만스러운, 어찌할 바를 모르는
talk in circles 돌려 얘기하다
straightforward 솔직한, 직설적인, 간단한
with no intention of ~할 의도[의향] 없이
such a waste of time 완전히 시간 낭비인
process-oriented 과정 지향적인
rational 합리적인, 이성적인
goal-oriented 목표 지향적인

남자와 여자의 성격 차이

난 내 여자친구가 정말 좋다, 그리고 그녀도 날 많이 좋아한다. 그런데 가끔 그 애가 나더러 자기가 원하는 게 뭔지 모른다고 말할 때면 정말 답답해 미치겠다. 말을 안 해 주는데 내가 어떻게 알겠어? 돌려서 말하니 내가 알 턱이 있나. 그리고 나한테 조언을 부탁해 오면 난 정확하게 그녀가 무엇을 하면 좋을지 말해 준다. 그런데 나보고 너무 솔직하다고 뭐라 한다. 또 어떨 때는 살 것도 없으면서 쇼핑을 간다. 정말 시간 낭비 아닌가. 도대체 왜 살 것도 없는데 쇼핑을 가는 거지? 물론 남자는 이성적이고 목표 지향적인 반면 여자는 감성적이고 과정 지향적이라지만 그래도, 이건 정말 해도 해도 너무한 것 같다.

Sentence Building

talk in circles 돌려 얘기하다

Stop talking in circles and get to the point.
I hate it when my boss talks in circles and doesn't get to the point.

돌려 얘기하지 말고 정확하게 용건을 말해.
팀장이 빙빙 돌려 얘기하면서 요점 없이 말할 땐 진짜 신경질난다.

straightforward 솔직한, 직설적인, 간단한

Are you being straightforward with me right now?
I want to be straightforward with you about this.

너 지금 솔직하게 얘기하고 있는 거니?
이 일에 대해 가감 없이 자네에게 솔직하게 얘기하겠네.

with no intention of ~할 의도[의향] 없이

He bought a laptop with no intention of using it.
We went to the theme park with no intention of riding roller coasters.

그는 사용하지도 않을 거면서 노트북을 구매했다.
롤러코스터를 타진 않을 거지만 놀이공원으로 놀러 갔다.

such a waste of time 완전히 시간 낭비인

Playing video games is such a waste of time.
It's such a waste of time to do all of this work for nothing.

비디오 게임을 하는 것은 정말 시간 낭비다.
이 모든 수고가 헛수고였다니 정말 시간 낭비했네.

Let's talk about today's topic.

1 What drives you crazy about the opposite sex?

2 What is the worst date you've ever been on?

3 Can men and women just be friends without dating?

Practice Questions

아래의 해석과 같은 의미가 되도록 빈칸을 채워 보세요.

1 I get really _____ when my baby won't stop crying.
우리 아기가 계속 울어대면 정말 어찌할 바를 모르겠어요.

2 Jack is _____ by nature.
잭은 천성적으로 목표 지향적인 사람이다.

3 That's a _____ argument.
그것 참 합리적인 주장이네.

괄호 안의 어휘를 이용하여 영작해 보세요.

4 돌려 얘기하지 말고 정확하게 용건을 말해. (talk in circles)
_____

5 너 지금 솔직하게 얘기하고 있는 거니? (straightforward)
_____

6 비디오 게임을 하는 것은 정말 시간 낭비다. (such a waste of time)
_____

Answers
❶ frustrated ❷ goal-oriented ❸ rational ❹ Stop talking in circles and get to the point.
❺ Are you being straightforward with me right now? ❻ Playing video games is such a waste of time.

Vocabulary Builder

빈칸에 들어갈 어휘를 상자 안에서 골라 적어 보세요.

> **frustrated**: disappointed or annoyed
>
> **straightforward**: direct and honest
>
> **intention**: to show one's purpose in their actions
>
> **process-oriented**: focus on the process of things
>
> **rational**: good sense and agreeable

1 Try to be _____ with your boss if there's a problem.

2 Leaders have to be _____ people to make good decisions.

3 I get _____ when I don't understand something right away.

4 It wasn't my _____ to offend you.

5 I like to think I'm a _____ person.

Answers

❶ straightforward ❷ rational ❸ frustrated ❹ intention ❺ process-oriented

My looks

소리 내어 읽고 해석해 보세요.

Jenny Is there anything that you want to change about your **looks**?

Craig Well, I wish I had **broader** shoulders and six-pack abs and also more hair. What about you?

Jenny Oh, I have so many things that I want to change. I wish my waist was thinner and my nose was smaller. And I **would give anything to** get rid of the **freckles** on my face.

Craig Wow, there are so many things you want to change. Is there anything that you like about your looks?

Jenny Why don't YOU tell me? What do you like about my looks?

Craig I like your **dimples** and your **natural flowing hair** and big pretty eyes.

Jenny Craig, **you know how to make a girl smile**.

> **Vocabulary**
>
> **looks** 외모, 모습, 표정
> **broad** 넓은
> **would give anything to** ~하기 위해서라면 무엇이든 다 할 용의가 있다
> **freckle** 주근깨
> **dimple** 보조개
> **natural flowing hair** 자연스럽게 흘러내리는 머리[머리카락]
> **you know how to make a girl[guy] + 형용사**
> 당신은 여자[남자]가 ~한 기분을 느끼게 만들 줄 안다

외모

Jenny   너 외모 중에 바꾸고 싶은 부분 있어?

Craig   음, 어깨가 좀 더 넓었으면 좋겠고 복근도 있었으면 좋겠고 머리숱도 더 많았으면 좋을 것 같아. 넌?

Jenny   아, 나도 바꾸고 싶은 곳이 엄청 많지. 허리가 좀 더 날씬했으면 좋겠고 코는 좀 더 작았으면 좋겠어. 그리고 얼굴에 주근깨만 없앨 수 있다면 뭐든 다 할 거야.

Craig   우와, 정말 바꾸고 싶은 게 많구나. 네 외모 중에 마음에 드는 부분은 없어?

Jenny   네가 한번 말해 줘 봐. 내 외모 중에 어디가 마음에 드니?

Craig   난 네 보조개랑 부드럽게 흘러내리는 머리카락 그리고 예쁘고 큰 눈이 좋아.

Jenny   크레이그, 넌 여자를 웃게 할 줄 아는 남자구나.

Sentence Building

looks 외모, 모습, 표정

Are you happy with your looks?
What's more important, looks or personality?

넌 너의 외모가 마음에 드니?
뭐가 더 중요하니, 외모 아니면 성격?

would give anything to
~하기 위해서라면 무엇이든 다 할 용의가 있다

I would give anything to have some peace and quiet at home.
I know Ken would give anything to get Jane back.

난 우리 집이 평온하고 조용해질 수만 있다면 뭐든지 하겠어.
켄은 제인과 다시 사귈 수만 있다면 뭐든지 다 할 수 있을 거야.

natural flowing hair 자연스럽게 흘러내리는 머리[머리카락]

Julia has such awesome natural flowing hair.
I think you would look better with natural flowing hair.

줄리아의 머리카락은 정말 자연스럽게 흘러내려서 예쁘다.
넌 자연스럽게 흘러내리는 머리를 하면 더 잘 어울릴 것 같아.

you know how to make a girl[guy] + 형용사
당신은 여자[남자]가 ~한 기분을 느끼게 만들 줄 안다

Oh, Bobby. You know how to make a girl blush.
You know how to make a guy feel special.

오, 바비. 당신은 여자를 참 당황하게 만드는군요.
당신은 남자를 다룰 줄 알아.

Let's talk about today's topic.

1. What are two things you would change about your looks?

2. What are some physical qualities you find attractive/unattractive?

3. Do you think plastic surgery is a good idea to change our looks?

Practice Questions

아래의 해석과 같은 의미가 되도록 빈칸을 채워 보세요.

1 It's almost impossible to get _____ in a week.
   1주일 만에 복근을 만든다는 것은 거의 불가능하다.

2 Pippi Longstocking has a face full of _____.
   말괄량이 삐삐는 얼굴이 주근깨 투성이야.

3 My daughter has the world's sweetest _____.
   내 딸아이의 보조개는 세상에서 제일 예쁘답니다.

괄호 안의 어휘를 이용하여 영작해 보세요.

4 넌 너의 외모가 마음에 드니? (looks)

   _____

5 켄은 제인과 다시 사귈 수만 있다면 뭐든지 다 할 수 있을 거야.
   (would give anything to)

   _____

6 줄리아의 머리카락은 정말 자연스럽게 흘러내려서 예쁘다.
   (natural flowing hair)

   _____

Answers
❶ six-pack abs ❷ freckles ❸ dimples ❹ Are you happy with your looks? ❺ I know Ken would give anything to get Jane back. ❻ Julia has such awesome natural flowing hair.

Vocabulary Builder

빈칸에 들어갈 어휘를 상자 안에서 골라 적어 보세요.

> **looks**: the appearance of a person
>
> **six-pack abs**: the greatly-developed muscles of a man's stomach
>
> **freckles**: dots on one's body
>
> **dimples**: small places where the skin creases

1 Emma's _____ on her face make her look so cute!

2 I want to laser off these _____ on my forehead.

3 What do you like most about my _____?

4 I've been working out, so now I have _____.

Answers
❶ dimples ❷ freckles ❸ looks ❹ six-pack abs

Plastic surgeries

소리 내어 읽고 해석해 보세요.

When I watch TV these days, I always wonder if there are any celebrities who haven't had plastic surgery. I understand how they must **feel pressured** to look better all the time, but I think **it's just too much**, especially when they look all the same. Some people may argue it's their own choice and as long as they look good **there's nothing to complain about**. Well, you can call me **old-fashioned**, but I think we've just **gone too far**. **Lookism** can cause some serious issues in a person's life. I think we all need to start looking at ourselves more sincerely and realize we can be better and healthier without **relying on cosmetic** procedures. I'm sorry if I sound too much like an old man, but I hope people will take this issue more seriously.

Vocabulary

feel pressured 압박감[부담감]을 느끼다
it's just too much. 이건 좀 너무 심하다[과하다]
there's nothing to complain about 불평할 게 전혀 없다, 불만이 없다
old-fashioned 구식의, 구식 사고방식을 지닌
gone too far 정도를 넘어선, 너무 지나친
lookism 외모지상주의
rely on ~에 의지[의존]하다, ~에 기대다
cosmetic 화장품, 미용의, 성형의

성형수술

요즘 TV에 나오는 연예인들을 보면 도대체 성형수술을 안 한 사람이 있기는 한 걸까 하는 생각이 든다. 물론 그들이 대중에게 항상 더 나은 모습을 보여 줘야 한다는 압박감에 시달리고 있다는 건 알지만, 이건 좀 심하다는 생각이 든다. 특히 얼굴이 죄다 똑같이 생긴 걸 볼 때면 말이다. 어떤 사람들은 성형은 단지 선택의 문제라고 보기 좋으면 그만이지 가타부타 말이 많냐고 할지도 모르겠다. 글쎄, 내가 구식이라 그런지는 몰라도 지금의 세태는 도를 넘어선 것 같다. 외모지상주의는 삶에 큰 문제들을 야기할 수 있다. 이젠 우리가 스스로에 대해서 더 진지하게 성찰하고 성형수술 따위에 의존하지 않아도 더 건강하고 멋진 삶을 살 수 있다는 걸 깨달아야 하지 않을까. 내가 너무 늙은이처럼 말하고 있다는 건 알지만, 사람들이 이 문제에 대해서 좀 더 심각하게 바라봤으면 좋겠다.

Sentence Building

feel pressured 압박감[부담감]을 느끼다

I feel pressured from my mom to always get good grades.
Do you feel pressured to get married?

항상 성적을 잘 받아야 한다고 우리 엄마에게 압박 받고 있어.
넌 결혼에 대한 압박감이 있니?

it's just too much 이건 좀 너무 심하다[과하다]

It's just too much to handle.
It's time to make it stop. It's just too much!

이건 감당하기 너무 힘들어.
이쯤에서 멈춰야 해. 이건 너무 심하잖아!

there's nothing to complain about
불평할 게 전혀 없다, 불만이 없다

There's nothing to complain about when you get everything you want.
The only complaint is there's nothing to complain about.

원하는 걸 다 얻었는데 뭘 불평하겠어.
유일한 불만은 불평할 게 하나도 없다는 거지.

gone too far 정도를 넘어선, 너무 지나친

By saying that joke, you've gone too far.
Individualism has gone too far in our society.

그 농담은 너무 지나쳤어.
이 사회의 개인주의는 정도를 넘어섰다.

Let's talk about today's topic.

1. Have you ever had or considered getting plastic surgery?

2. What is the most common surgery? Why is it so common?

3. Are there downsides to getting plastic surgery?

Practice Questions

아래의 해석과 같은 의미가 되도록 빈칸을 채워 보세요.

1 What are your thoughts on _____?
외모지상주의에 대한 너의 의견은 어때?

2 Plastic surgery can be either _____ or reconstructive.
성형수술은 미용수술일 수도 있고 재건수술일 수도 있지.

3 My dad is too _____.
우리 아빠는 너무 구식이에요.

괄호 안의 어휘를 이용하여 영작해 보세요.

4 넌 결혼에 대한 압박감이 있니? (feel pressured)
_____

5 이건 감당하기 너무 힘들어. (it's just too much)
_____

6 이 사회의 개인주의는 정도를 넘어섰다. (gone too far)
_____

Answers
❶ lookism ❷ cosmetic ❸ old-fashioned ❹ Do you feel pressured to get married?
❺ It's just too much to handle. ❻ Individualism has gone too far in our society.

Vocabulary Builder

빈칸에 들어갈 어휘를 상자 안에서 골라 적어 보세요.

> **celebrity**: someone who is very famous, especially in the entertainment business
>
> **old-fashioned**: prefer the times of the past
>
> **lookism**: discriminate someone because of their looks
>
> **rely on**: needing someone or something to do an action
>
> **cosmetic**: makeup products

1. Dad, your thinking is so _____.

2. I need to go to the store to get a certain face _____.

3. I don't agree with the idea of _____.

4. You'll have to _____ me to get into the club.

5. Is the President considered a _____?

Answers
❶ old-fashioned ❷ cosmetic ❸ lookism ❹ rely on ❺ celebrity

Unit 07 Meeting people through online dating sites

소리 내어 읽고 해석해 보세요.

June Have you ever met a girl through online sites or dating apps?

William Yes, I have. **As a matter of fact**, those are the only ways I meet girls these days.

June Oh, really? Do you see their pictures first before you **meet them in person**?

William Of course I do because I don't want to **take any chances**. But sometimes those pictures can be very **misleading**. They **edit** their pictures so much.

June Haha. I'm sure they do.

William How about you, June? Have you ever done online dating?

June Just once. And it was a disaster.

William Why? What happened?

June He sounded so nice at first, but **later on**, he asked me if I could lend him some money. So, I stopped talking to that guy. I think he was a **fraud**.

Vocabulary

as a matter of fact 사실은, 실은, 솔직히 말하면
meet someone in person ~을 실제로 만나다, 직접 만나다
take chances 위험한 선택[행동]을 하다, 요행을 바라다, 운에 맡기고 해 보다
misleading 호도하는, 오해의 소지가 있는
edit 편집하다
later on 나중에
fraud 사기, 사기꾼

온라인 만남

June 온라인 사이트나 데이트 주선 앱을 통해서 여자를 만나 본 적 있어?

William 응, 있어. 솔직히 말하면, 요즘 내가 여자를 만나는 방법이 그것밖에는 없어.

June 아, 정말? 실제로 만나기 전에 사진부터 봐?

William 당연하지, 자칫하다가 폭탄 맞을 수도 있으니까. 근데 어떨 때는 사진만 믿었다가 큰코다칠 때도 있어. 사진 편집을 장난 아니게 하거든.

June 하하. 당연히 그렇겠지.

William 넌 어때, 준? 너도 온라인 통해서 남자를 만나 본 적 있어?

June 딱 한 번. 근데 완전 최악이었어.

William 왜? 어떻게 됐는데?

June 처음에는 꽤 괜찮은 사람인 줄 알았는데, 나중에는 나한테 돈을 빌려 달라는 거야. 그래서, 대화를 끊어 버렸지. 아무래도 그놈 사기꾼이었던 것 같아.

Sentence Building

as a matter of fact 사실은, 실은, 솔직히 말하면

As a matter of fact, I do enjoy mountain climbing.
As a matter of fact, I've never been here in my life.

사실은 나도 등산 많이 좋아해.
사실은 나 여기에 와 본 적이 없어.

meet in person ~을 실제로 만나다, 직접 만나다

I don't think we should buy this until we meet him in person.
If you met her in person, you would believe me.

그를 직접 만나기 전까지는 이걸 사면 안 될 것 같아.
그녀를 네가 직접 만나 보면, 내 말을 믿을 거야.

take chances
위험한 선택[행동]을 하다, 요행을 바라다, 운에 맡기고 해 보다

I like to take chances when I'm doing extreme sports.
I would never take chances with my children's health.

난 익스트림 스포츠를 할 때는 위험을 감수하는 것을 좋아한다.
난 절대 우리 아이들의 건강을 운에 맡기는 짓은 안 할 거야.

later on 나중에

Later on we're going to go to the club, ok?
He's going to tell me about his experiences later on today.

있다가 우리 클럽에 갈 거지, 응?
오늘 나중에 그가 그의 경험들에 대해 이야기해 줄 거야.

 **Let's talk about today's topic.**

1 Have you ever used a dating site to get a date?

2 Why has online dating become so popular these days?

3 What could be the next step after online dating?

Practice Questions

아래의 해석과 같은 의미가 되도록 빈칸을 채워 보세요.

1 The article is _____.
그 기사는 오해의 소지가 있다.

2 It turned out he was a _____.
그는 알고 보니 사기꾼이었어.

3 _____, I've never been here in my life.
사실은 나 여기에 와 본 적이 없어.

괄호 안의 어휘를 이용하여 영작해 보세요.

4 그녀를 네가 직접 만나 보면 내 말을 믿을 거야. (meet in person)
_____

5 난 절대 우리 아이들의 건강을 운에 맡기는 짓은 안 할 거야. (take chances)
_____

6 오늘 나중에 그가 그의 경험들에 대해 이야기해 줄 거야. (later on)
_____

Answers
❶ misleading ❷ fraud ❸ as a matter of fact ❹ If you met her in person, you would believe me. ❺ I would never take chances with my children's health. ❻ He's going to tell me about his experiences later on today.

Vocabulary Builder

빈칸에 들어갈 어휘를 상자 안에서 골라 적어 보세요.

> **misleading**: not completely truthful
>
> **edit**: change something
>
> **at first**: for the first time
>
> **fraud**: when someone tricks you

1 I had to _____ some of your essay to make it sound better.

2 I think this advertisement is a little _____.

3 _____ I couldn't believe anything he was saying.

4 He's a _____ if he promises one thing, and delivers another.

Answers
❶ edit ❷ misleading ❸ At first ❹ fraud

Ever been in a relationship with a younger man/ an older woman?

소리 내어 읽고 해석해 보세요.

I have a boyfriend who is five years younger than me. I know he's a bit young for me but people say I **look very young for my age** and I'm **young at heart**, so we seem to **get along** great. But **the thing is**, he's still in college and I already have a job, which, **in other words**, means that he has no money and I have to pay for almost everything when we go out on a date. Although I always tell him it's not a problem at all, honestly, I'm not really okay with it. Sometimes I feel like he's still a baby. I think dating a younger guy has its benefits but there are some **drawbacks**. **On second thought**, maybe I should start dating someone **my own age**, or even older.

Vocabulary

look young for one's age 나이보다 젊어[어려] 보이다
young at heart 마음은 청춘
get along (with) (~와) 잘 지내다, 사이 좋게 지내다
in other words 다시 말해서
the thing is (중요한 사실, 이유를 언급하려고 할 때) 문제는, 실은
drawback 결점, 문제점
on second thought 다시 생각해 보니, 잘 생각해 보니
one's own age ~와 같은 나이, 동갑

연하남/연상녀와 사귄 적이 있나요?

내 남자친구는 나보다 다섯 살이 어리다. 좀 나이 차이가 나긴 하지만 사람들이 내가 나이보다 훨씬 더 어려 보인다고 하기도 하고 내 사고방식이 어려서 우린 잘 맞는 구석이 참 많다. 그런데 문제는, 걔는 아직 대학생이고 난 이미 직장인, 그러니까 다시 말해, 남자친구가 돈이 없어 데이트 비용을 내가 거의 다 감당해야 한다는 것. 물론 난 늘 괜찮다고 말하지만, 솔직히 괜찮지 않다. 어떨 때는 남자친구가 완전 아기 같기도 하다. 연하를 만나는 게 좋은 점도 있긴 하지만 문제도 많은 듯하다. 다시 생각해 보니, 어쩌면 동갑이나 연상을 만나는 것도 나쁘진 않은 것 같다.

Sentence Building

look young for one's age 나이보다 젊어[어려] 보이다

Man, that girl really looks young for her age.
I like it when people tell me I look young for my age.

와, 저 여자 정말 나이보다 어려 보인다.
사람들이 나한테 나이보다 어려 보인다고 하면 기분 좋더라.

young at heart 마음은 청춘

Even though I'm older, I'm young at heart.
Feeling young at heart may help you live longer.

내 나이가 더 많을 수는 있지만, 마음만은 청춘이야.
마음이 젊으면 더 오래 살 수도 있지.

the thing is (중요한 사실, 이유를 언급하려고 할 때) 문제는, 실은

The thing is, I can't ride the rollercoaster because I'm scared.
The thing is, they turned me down.

실은, 난 무서워서 롤러코스터 못 타.
실은, 그들이 나를 거부했어.

on second thought 다시 생각해 보니, 잘 생각해 보니

On second thought, maybe I would like to have another cookie.
On second thought, he may be the wrong person to ask.

다시 생각해 보니, 나 과자 하나 더 먹을래.
잘 생각해 보니, 아무래도 그 사람한테 물어보는 건 아닌 것 같아.

Let's talk about today's topic.

1. What is the largest age gap you've had with a boy/girlfriend?

2. Is it possible to date someone with more than a 10 year age difference?

3. What are the positives to dating younger/older people?

Practice Questions

아래의 해석과 같은 의미가 되도록 빈칸을 채워 보세요.

1 There are many _____ to living in the city.
도시에 사는 것에는 결점이 많다.

2 Meet someone _____.
네 또래[동갑]하고 만나라.

3 I like it when people tell me I _____
_____.
사람들이 나한테 나이보다 어려 보인다고 하면 기분 좋더라.

괄호 안의 어휘를 이용하여 영작해 보세요.

4 내 나이가 더 많을 수는 있지만, 마음만은 청춘이야. (young at heart)
_____

5 실은, 그들이 나를 거부했어. (the thing is)
_____

6 잘 생각해 보니, 아무래도 그 사람한테 물어보는 건 아닌 것 같아.
(on second thought)
_____

Answers
❶ drawbacks ❷ your own age ❸ look young for my age ❹ Even though I'm older, I'm young at heart. ❺ The thing is, they turned me down. ❻ On second thought, he may be the wrong person to ask.

Vocabulary Builder

빈칸에 들어갈 어휘를 상자 안에서 골라 적어 보세요.

> **get along**: be able to be around each other
>
> **in other words**: to say it a different way
>
> **drawback**: a negative aspect
>
> **one's own age**: a person's age

1. The _____ of living in a big house is the higher utility fees.

2. _____, we can't go because of the bad weather.

3. I'm able to _____ with my colleagues at work really well.

4. She needs friends _____.

Answers
❶ drawback ❷ In other words ❸ get along ❹ her own age

Ever been in a relationship with a player?

소리 내어 읽고 해석해 보세요.

A couple of weeks ago, I was in the Hongdae area walking down the street. And this one guy **came up to me** and asked me if I had time to talk. Normally, I would not **get involved with** a guy like that. But I could **tell by the look on his face** that he was sincere. So, we **got to talking** and **one thing led to another** and now we are **officially going out**. But **the trouble is** all my friends tell me that he's a player. You know why? Because he never talks about his personal life and he often goes outside to take phone calls when he's with me. But that doesn't make him a player. I think my friends are just **jealous** because he's so cute and sweet. If he was a player, he wouldn't treat me so nice and even sing for me over the phone every night, would he?

Vocabulary

come up to someone ~에게 다가가다
get involved with ~와 관계를 갖다, 연루되다
tell by the look on one's face ~의 표정을 보고 알아차리다
got to talking 대화를 시작하다, 이야기의 물꼬가 터지다
one thing leads to another 꼬리를 물로 상황이 자연스럽게 이어지다, 어쩌다 보니 상황이 어떤 방향으로 전개되다(사귀게 되거나 잠자리를 하게 될 때)
officially going out 공식적으로 사귀는
the trouble is (that) 난처하게도, 문제는
jealous 질투하는, 시샘하는

바람둥이와 사귄 적이 있나요?

몇 주 전 홍대 근처를 배회하고 있었는데 말이야. 어떤 남자애가 다가와서 얘기 좀 할 수 있는지 묻더라고. 보통은 그런 식으로 길거리에서 여자한테 말 거는 남자하고는 상종을 안 해. 그런데 그 남자애는 왠지 그냥 딱 봐도 진솔해 보였어. 그래서 이런저런 얘기를 나누기 시작했고. 어쩌다 보니 이미 우리는 공식커플이 되어 버렸지. 그런데 문제는, 내 친구들이 하나같이 그 남자애가 바람둥이래. 그 이유가 뭔지 알아? 걔가 절대 자기 사생활에 관해 얘기 안 하고 나랑 만날 때 자꾸 밖에 나가서 전화를 받고 그런다고. 도대체 그게 바람둥이랑 무슨 상관이지? 아무래도 게네들이 내 남자친구가 귀엽고 착하니까 완전 질투하는 것 같아. 바람둥이였다면 나한테 그렇게 잘하고 매일 밤 전화해서 노래도 불러 주고 그렇겠어, 설마?

Sentence Building

tell by the look on one's face ~의 표정을 보고 알아차리다

I can tell by the look on her face that she hated my present.
It was easy to tell by the look on his face.

그녀의 표정을 보면 내 선물이 마음에 들지 않는다는 것을 알 수 있어.
그의 얼굴 표정만 봐도 딱 알겠더라고.

got to talking 대화를 시작하다, 이야기의 물꼬가 터지다

My buddy and I got to talking and we decided to go to Canada.
The other day, my uncle Ted and I got to talking about life.

친구하고 이런저런 이야기를 하다가 우리는 결국 캐나다로 가기로 결정했다.
요전에, 테드 삼촌하고 나하고 인생에 대해서 이런저런 이야기를 나눴어.

one thing led to another
꼬리를 물로 상황이 자연스럽게 이어지다, 어쩌다 보니 상황이 어떤 방향으로 전개되다
(사귀게 되거나 잠자리를 하게 될 때)

I was with this guy and one thing led to another.
One thing led to another and we ended up kissing.

어떤 남자를 만났는데 상황이 점점 발전하더라고.
점점 상황이 이상하게 전개되더니만 결국 우리는 키스를 하고 말았지.

the trouble is (that) 난처하게도, 문제는

The trouble is I don't have enough money for the trip.
The trouble is she doesn't know my number.

문제는 내겐 여행을 갈 돈이 없다는 거야.
문제는 그녀가 내 전화번호를 모른다는 거지.

Let's talk about today's topic.

1 Have you ever dated a player?

2 How can you tell if someone is a player?

3 What would you say to your friend if you found out he/she was dating a player?

Practice Questions

아래의 해석과 같은 의미가 되도록 빈칸을 채워 보세요.

1 Irene and I are _____.
아이린과 나는 이제 공식적인 커플이야.

2 Don't _____ a married man.
유부남과는 사귀지 말아라.

3 Everyone knows that he's a _____.
그가 바람둥이라는 것은 모두가 다 알아.

괄호 안의 어휘를 이용하여 영작해 보세요.

4 그의 얼굴 표정만 봐도 딱 알겠더라고. (tell by the look on one's face)
_____

5 점점 상황이 이상하게 전개되더니만 결국 우리는 키스를 하고 말았지.
(one thing led to another)
_____

6 문제는 내겐 여행을 갈 돈이 없다는 거야. (the trouble is)
_____

Answers

❶ officially going out ❷ get involved with ❸ player ❹ It was easy to tell by the look on his face. ❺ One thing led to another and we ended up kissing. ❻ The trouble is I don't have enough money for the trip.

Vocabulary Builder

빈칸에 들어갈 어휘를 상자 안에서 골라 적어 보세요.

> **come up to**: approach
>
> **normally**: generally
>
> **get involved with**: start dating
>
> **player**: someone who is in a relationship with various people
>
> **jealous**: feeling slightly angry because of a rivalry

1 I'm so _____ you got a gift and I didn't.

2 _____ I go to the store on Saturdays.

3 Josh is such a _____. I saw him with three different girls last week.

4 If they _____ you, just ignore them. They want to fight.

5 I like to _____ nice guys.

Answers
❶ jealous ❷ Normally ❸ player ❹ come up to ❺ get involved with

Unit 10 Who pays when on a date?

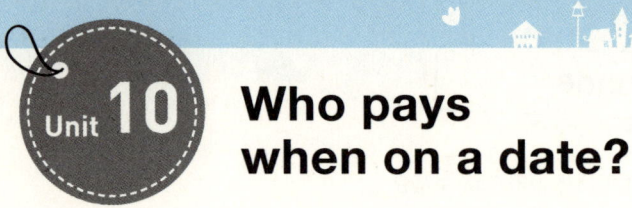

소리 내어 읽고 해석해 보세요.

Rudy Why do guys always have to pay for everything when we're on a date?

Kayla You pay for everything? Why would you do that?

Rudy Because the girls that I date **wouldn't pay a penny** out of their pockets.

Kayla Where do you even meet these girls? That's **ridiculous**.

Rudy Exactly! I mean, if I buy dinner, they should at least pay for coffee.

Kayla I always **pay for my share**.

Rudy You mean, you pay 50% of the **bill**?

Kayla Yeah, of course, especially when I'm on a blind date. I don't want to **feel like I owe him something**.

Rudy Kayla, you are SO **my type!**

Vocabulary

wouldn't pay a penny 십 원도 안 내려고 하다
penny 1센트
ridiculous 말도 안 되는, 터무니없는
pay for one's share 자신의 몫[부담금]을 내다
bill 계산서, 청구서
feel like + 주어 + owe someone something ~에게 ~을 빚진 것 같은 기분이 들다
one's type ~가 좋아하는 타입, 취향, 이상형

데이트 비용은 누가 내나요?

Rudy   왜 데이트할 때는 남자가 돈을 다 내야 하는 거야?

Kayla   네가 다 내니? 왜 그런 짓을 해?

Rudy   나랑 데이트하는 여자들은 절대 자기 주머니에서는 십 원도 안 꺼내려고 하니까 그렇지.

Kayla   넌 그런 여자들을 도대체 어디서 만나는 거니? 정말 어이없네.

Rudy   내 말이! 내가 밥을 사면 적어도 커피 정도는 사야지.

Kayla   난 항상 내가 먹은 건 내가 내는데.

Rudy   뭐야, 반반씩 계산한단 말이야?

Kayla   음, 당연하지, 특히 소개팅에 나갔을 땐 더 그렇고. 빚진 것 같은 기분이 별로거든.

Rudy   케일라. 너 완전 내 스타일이야!

Sentence Building

wouldn't pay a penny 십 원도 안 내려고 하다

If I didn't agree with the policy, I wouldn't pay a penny.
I wouldn't pay a penny for a book like that.

내가 그 규정에 동조할 수 없다면, 난 십 원도 낼 생각이 없다.
그런 책에는 난 십 원도 지불할 생각이 없어.

pay for one's share 자신의 몫[부담금]을 내다

Hey, I'll pay for my share when I get my paycheck on Friday.
You will need to pay for your share of the cost.

야, 금요일에 월급 나오면 나도 내 몫을 낼 거야.
비용 중에서 네 몫은 너도 내야 할 거야.

feel like + 주어 + owe someone something
~에게 ~을 빚진 것 같은 기분이 들다

He's been so nice, I feel like I owe him so much.
Don't ever feel like you owe me anything.

그 사람이 너무 잘 해 줘서, 나중에 크게 갚아야만 할 것 같아.
절대로 나한테 빚졌다고 생각하지 마.

one's type ~가 좋아하는 타입, 취향, 이상형

Hailey is so my type.
He's just not my type.

헤일리가 내 이상형이야.
그는 내 취향이 전혀 아니야.

Let's talk about today's topic.

1 Who pays when you are on a date? Why?

2 Should there be strict rules on etiquette when dating?

3 What is the worst date you've ever been on?

Practice Questions

아래의 해석과 같은 의미가 되도록 빈칸을 채워 보세요.

1 What you're saying is _____.
네가 하는 말은 터무니없다.

2 Did you see my phone _____?
내 통신비 고지서 봤니?

3 He's been so nice, I _____ so much.
그 사람이 너무 잘 해 줘서, 나중에 크게 갚아야만 할 것 같아.

괄호 안의 어휘를 이용하여 영작해 보세요.

4 그런 책에는 난 십 원도 지불할 생각이 없어. (wouldn't pay a penny)

_____

5 비용 중에서 네 몫은 너도 내야 할 거야. (pay for one's share)

_____

6 헤일리가 내 이상형이야. (one's type)

_____

Answers
❶ ridiculous ❷ bill ❸ feel like I owe him ❹ I wouldn't pay a penny for a book like that.
❺ You will need to pay for your share of the cost. ❻ Hailey is so my type.

Vocabulary Builder

빈칸에 들어갈 어휘를 상자 안에서 골라 적어 보세요.

> **penny**: 1 cent
>
> **ridiculous**: absurd
>
> **one's share**: the amount one owes
>
> **owe**: how much you have to repay

1 I don't even have a _____.

2 Everybody has to pay _____ when the check comes.

3 What? It's _____ to pay double the price online.

4 How much do I _____ you guys?

Answers
❶ penny ❷ one's share ❸ ridiculous ❹ owe

69

Unit 11	**Embarrassing drunk nights**
	술자리 실수 경험
Unit 12	**Memorable gifts**
	기억에 남는 선물
Unit 13	**Dream wedding**
	꿈의 결혼식
Unit 14	**Breakfast**
	아침 식사
Unit 15	**Do you cook?**
	요리하세요?
Unit 16	**Grocery shopping**
	장보기
Unit 17	**Food shows on TV**
	TV 먹방
Unit 18	**School uniforms**
	교복
Unit 19	**Study groups**
	스터디 모임
Unit 20	**Social clubs**
	동호회

Part 2

Unit 11 — Embarrassing drunk nights

소리 내어 읽고 해석해 보세요.

I like drinking but not with those who have obnoxious drinking habits. You know how there are people who change **drastically** when they are drunk. I **can't stand the guys** who start **weeping (if not wailing)** when they **get buzzed**. Worse are those who keep repeating what they say **over and over again**. You know what the worst is though, girls who laugh hysterically and slap me on the back so hard it **takes the wind out of me**. Damn, please, stop doing that! But there are some girls with cute habits I wouldn't mind being a victim of. Like those who flirt with a little bit of physical contact without making it too obvious. But I can't enjoy it too much because I always **fall asleep** after drinking just two shots of soju.

Vocabulary

drastically 극단적으로, 급격하게
can't stand someone[something] ~을 견딜 수가 없다, ~가 너무 싫다
weep 울다, 눈물을 흘리다
if not + (앞부분의 상황보다 더 심한 상황) 심지어는 ~일 수도 있는
wail 울부짖다, 통곡하다
get buzzed 술기운이 오르다, 취하다
over and over again 여러 번 반복해서
take the wind out of someone 거의 숨이 멎을 지경이 되게 하다
fall asleep 잠이 들다

술자리 실수 경험

난 술 마시는 것을 좋아하지만 술버릇이 고약한 사람들과 마시는 것은 싫다. 술만 마시면 성격이 180도 바뀌는 그런 사람들 말이다. 취하면 꺼이꺼이 울기 시작하는 (아예 대성통곡하는 사람들도 있고) 그런 부류의 사람들도 정말 싫다. 했던 말을 또 하고 또 하는 사람들은 더 싫다. 그런데 그보다 더 견디기 힘든 건, 별로 웃기지도 않은데 미친 사람처럼 박장대소하면서 내 등을 후려치는 여자들인데, 너무 세게 때려서 숨이 꽉 막혀 버릴 지경이다. 제발, 그만 좀 하라고! 하지만 가끔은 당해도 좋을 정도로 주사가 귀엽게 느껴지는 여자들도 있다. 너무 눈에 띄지 않을 정도의 끼를 부리면서 약간의 신체 접촉을 유도하는 그런 유형의 여자들. 그러나 소주 두 잔만 마셔도 바로 인사불성이 되어 버리는 나는 아쉬울 따름이다.

Sentence Building

can't stand someone[something]
~을 견딜 수가 없다, ~가 너무 싫다

I just can't stand Jeremy! He's such a jerk!
I can't stand working with him anymore!

제러미 왕 짜증이야! 재수 없는 놈!
그 사람하고 더 이상 같이 일 못하겠어!

if not + (앞부분의 상황보다 더 심한 상황) 심지어는 ~일 수도 있는

Jack must be dying, if not dead already.
It will cost you at least $1000, if not more.

잭은 지금 죽어 가고 있을걸, 이미 죽지 않았다면 말이지.
천 달러는 들 거야, 더 많이 들 수도 있고.

over and over again 여러 번 반복해서

Why do we have to study this over and over again?
I tried it over and over again.

우리가 왜 이걸 계속 반복해서 공부해야 하는 거죠?
하고 또 하고 여러 번 반복해서 시도했어.

take the wind out of someone
거의 숨이 멎을 지경이 되게 하다

When I climb the mountain, it really takes the wind out of me.
That punch really took the wind out of me.

등산하면 숨이 차서 죽을 것 같아.
그 펀치에 숨이 멎을 뻔했어.

Let's talk about today's topic.

1 Have you had any memorable drunk nights?

2 How do you think the drinking culture in Korea is different than other countries?

3 What is an action or situation you dislike while drinking?

Practice Questions

아래의 해석과 같은 의미가 되도록 빈칸을 채워 보세요.

1 My life _____ changed in 2015.
내 인생은 2015년도에 급격하게 변했어.

2 I'm getting _____.
아, 취한다.

3 I _____ working with him anymore!
그 사람하고 더 이상 같이 일 못하겠어!

괄호 안의 어휘를 이용하여 영작해 보세요.

4 천 달러는 들 거야, 더 많이 들 수도 있고. (if not)
_____

5 우리가 왜 이걸 계속 반복해서 공부해야 하는 거죠? (over and over again)
_____

6 그 펀치에 숨이 멎을 뻔했어. (take the wind out of)
_____

Answers
❶ drastically ❷ buzzed ❸ can't stand ❹ It will cost you at least $1000, if not more.
❺ Why do we have to study this over and over again? ❻ That punch really took the wind out of me.

Vocabulary Builder

빈칸에 들어갈 어휘를 상자 안에서 골라 적어 보세요.

> **drastically**: extremely
>
> **weep**: to cry a lot
>
> **wail**: to cry in a loud high voice
>
> **get buzzed**: feeling light-headed when drinking
>
> **fall asleep**: to go to sleep

1 It's so annoying to hear the baby next door _____.

2 Don't _____. It's only spilled milk.

3 When I went to the academy, my skills _____ improved.

4 I'm so tired I just want to go home and _____.

5 Only when I drink soju do I _____.

Answers
❶ wail ❷ weep ❸ drastically ❹ fall asleep ❺ get buzzed

Memorable gifts

소리 내어 읽고 해석해 보세요.

Lily What was **the most memorable gift** you've ever received from someone?

Victor Well, I've never thought about that. Give me some time to think. What about you? Have you received any memorable gifts?

Lily **Indeed**, I have. My boyfriend got me the cutest dog in the world for my 20th birthday. She is the most memorable gift I've gotten.

Victor **That must have been** a great gift. Oh, I just remembered a gift that I thought was very special.

Lily What is it?

Victor My very first car that my dad bought me when I got my driver's license.

Lily Wow! Your dad must be super rich.

Victor No, actually it was a very old **used car**, so it was like 1 million won. But I was so excited to own a car **for the first time in my life**!

Lily Good for you!

Vocabulary

the most memorable + 명사 가장 기억에 남는 것
indeed 참으로, 정말로, (긍정적인 진술, 대답을 강조하여) 정말
that must have been ~ 정말 ~했겠구나[였겠다]
used car 중고차
for the first time in my life 평생 처음으로

기억에 남는 선물

Lily 넌 지금까지 살면서 가장 기억에 남는 선물이 뭐야?

Victor 글쎄, 한 번도 생각해 본 적이 없는데. 잠깐 생각할 시간을 줘 봐. 넌 어떤데? 기억에 남는 선물이 있어?

Lily 나야 있지. 스무 살 생일에 남자친구가 세상에서 가장 귀여운 강아지를 선물로 줬거든. 그 강아지가 가장 기억에 남는 선물이야.

Victor 정말 멋진 선물이었겠다. 아, 나도 하나 아주 특별하다고 생각했던 선물이 기억났어.

Lily 뭔데?

Victor 내가 운전면허증 땄을 때 아빠가 사 주신 내 생애 첫 번째 차.

Lily 와! 너희 아빠 엄청 부자이신가 봐.

Victor 아냐, 사실은 한 백만 원 정도 하는 완전 낡은 중고차였어. 그래도 내 생애 첫 차라서 기분은 최고였지!

Lily 정말 좋았겠다!

Sentence Building

the most memorable + 명사 가장 기억에 남는 것

The most memorable vacation I've ever been on was to California.
What is the most memorable event in your life?

지금까지 휴가 중에 가장 기억에 남는 휴가는 캘리포니아에 갔었을 때야.
살면서 가장 기억에 남는 일이 뭐니?

indeed 참으로, 정말로, (긍정적인 진술, 대답을 강조하여) 정말

Indeed, paying double the price for a product is throwing away money.
That is indeed amazing.

정말이지, 물건 값을 두 배나 주고 사는 건 돈을 갖다 버리는 거나 마찬가지야.
참으로 놀랍도다.

that must have been ~ 정말 ~했겠구나[였겠다]

That must have been really difficult to eat all that food.
That party must have been a blast.

거기 있는 음식을 다 먹으려면 정말 힘들었겠구나.
그 파티 정말 재미있었겠네.

for the first time in my life 평생 처음으로

**For the first time in my life I finally understand what this means.
I feel alive for the first time in my life.**

내 평생 처음으로 이제서야 이게 무슨 뜻인지 알겠다.
평생 처음으로 살아 있는 것 같은 느낌이야.

Let's talk about today's topic.

1. What was the most memorable gift you've ever been given?

2. What is the worst gift you've ever received?

3. When is it ok to give gifts that are not on birthdays?

Practice Questions

아래의 해석과 같은 의미가 되도록 빈칸을 채워 보세요.

1 He's a _____ dealer.
그는 중고차 딜러야.

2 I'm going to be _____ in 10 years.
난 10년 후면 엄청난 부자가 될 거야.

3 What is the _____ event in your life?
넌 살면서 가장 기억에 남는 일이 뭐니?

괄호 안의 어휘를 이용하여 영작해 보세요.

4 참으로 놀랍도다. (indeed)
_____

5 그 파티 정말 재미있었겠네. (that must have been)
_____

6 평생 처음으로 살아 있는 것 같은 느낌이야. (for the first time in my life)
_____

Answers

❶ used car ❷ super rich ❸ most memorable ❹ That is indeed amazing. ❺ That party must have been a blast. ❻ I feel alive for the first time in my life.

Vocabulary Builder

빈칸에 들어갈 어휘를 상자 안에서 골라 적어 보세요.

> **memorable**: something special to remember
>
> **indeed**: fact or reality
>
> **used car**: a car that was owned by another person
>
> **super rich**: very, very rich

1 Johnny is _____ if he can afford that car.

2 My trip to Europe was the most _____ in my life.

3 I needed to save some money so I bought a _____.

4 It is _____ a crime to take an opened alcoholic beverage on the subway.

Answers
❶ super rich ❷ memorable ❸ used car ❹ indeed

Dream wedding

소리 내어 읽고 해석해 보세요.

Betty   I want to have a big wedding with all of my friends and family there, **if you ask me**.

Wayne   The way I feel is that a wedding is a very personal event. So, I want to have a very small wedding with only **immediate family**.

Betty   I think you can make it personal and still have a big wedding.

Wayne   Of course you can. I think it just has to do with my personality.

Betty   What does your girlfriend say about this?

Wayne   She always says that she's been **dreaming of** a fancy **garden wedding**.

Betty   A garden wedding sounds amazing! You know, a wedding is the most important event in the life of every woman. So, why don't you make her dream **come true**?

Wayne   I wish I could. But I **can't afford** it.

Betty   Think again. **If there's a will, there's a way.**

Vocabulary

if you ask me 내 생각에는, 내 의견을 말하자면
immediate family 직계가족
dream of ~을 꿈꾸다
garden wedding 가든 예식, 야외 결혼식
come true 이루어지다, 실현되다
if there's a will, there's a way 뜻이 있는 곳에 길이 있다
can't afford ~할 여유가 없다 (특히 금전적인 여유)

꿈의 결혼식

Betty   난 내 친구들하고 친척들 모두 초청해서 성대한 결혼식을 치르고 싶어. 네가 혹 궁금하다면 말이지.

Wayne   난 결혼식은 지극히 개인적인 일이라고 생각해. 그래서 직계가족만 모여서 조촐하게 하고 싶어.

Betty   개인적으로 하면서도 크게 할 수 있잖아.

Wayne   물론 그럴 수도 있겠지. 아마 그냥 내 성격 때문에 그런 것 같아.

Betty   네 여자친구는 이런 네 생각에 대해서 어떻게 생각하는데?

Wayne   내 여자친구는 화려하고 멋진 야외 결혼식을 늘 꿈꿔 왔대.

Betty   야외 결혼식 정말 멋지겠다! 너, 여자들에게 결혼식은 일생일대의 중대사라는 거 알지. 그러니까 그녀의 꿈을 이루어 주는 게 어때?

Wayne   나도 그렇게 하고 싶어. 그런데 능력이 안 돼.

Betty   다시 한 번 생각해 봐. 마음만 먹으면 세상에 못 할 건 없어.

Sentence Building

if you ask me 내 생각에는, 내 의견을 말하자면

This is totally ridiculous, if you ask me.
If you ask me, it's just an excuse.

내 생각을 굳이 듣길 원한다면, 이건 정말 어처구니없다.
내 의견을 말하자면, 이건 그저 핑계로 보인다.

dream of ~을 꿈꾸다

I've been dreaming of this day since I was a boy.
I've been dreaming of a white Christmas.

오늘은 내가 어릴 적부터 꿈꿔 오던 바로 그런 날이야.
난 화이트 크리스마스를 꿈꿔 왔어.

can't afford ~할 여유가 없다 (특히 금전적인 여유)

We can't afford to lose our customers to our competitors.
I can't afford to buy a new house.

우리에겐 고객들을 경쟁사에 빼앗겨도 될 만한 여유가 없다.
새 집을 살만한 돈이 없어.

if there's a will, there's a way 뜻이 있는 곳에 길이 있다

They say if there's a will, there's a way.
Do you believe in the saying, "if there's a will, there's a way"?

사람들이 말하기를 뜻이 있는 곳에 길이 있다고 하잖아.
'마음만 먹으면 뭐든 다 할 수 있다'는 말을 믿니?

Let's talk about today's topic.

1. What is a common wedding like in Korea? How does it differ from other countries?

2. Is there anything you want to change about Korean wedding culture?

3. What is your dream wedding like?

Practice Questions

아래의 해석과 같은 의미가 되도록 빈칸을 채워 보세요.

1 We've decided to invite only _____.
직계가족만 초대하기로 했다.

2 I wonder if my dreams would ever _____.
내 꿈이 이루어질지 모르겠다.

3 This is totally ridiculous, _____.
내 생각을 굳이 듣길 원한다면, 이건 정말 어처구니없다.

괄호 안의 어휘를 이용하여 영작해 보세요.

4 난 화이트 크리스마스를 꿈꿔 왔어. (dream of)

_____

5 새 집을 살 만한 돈이 없어. (can't afford)

_____

6 사람들이 말하기를 뜻이 있는 곳에 길이 있다고 하잖아.
(if there's a will, there's a way)

_____

Answers
❶ immediate family ❷ come true ❸ if you ask me ❹ I've been dreaming of a white Christmas. ❺ I can't afford to buy a new house. ❻ They say if there's a will, there's a way.

Vocabulary Builder

빈칸에 들어갈 어휘를 상자 안에서 골라 적어 보세요.

> **immediate family**: one's closest relations, such as parents, children, spouse
>
> **personal**: for only one person
>
> **come true**: to happen as hoped for
>
> **garden wedding**: a wedding in a garden

1. Please invite only _____ to the special ceremony.

2. All of my wishes had _____.

3. Please only use this for your _____ use.

4. I really want to have a _____ outside in the sunshine.

Answers
❶ immediate family ❷ come true ❸ personal ❹ garden wedding

Unit 14 Breakfast

소리 내어 읽고 해석해 보세요.

4:30A.M, the sound of the alarm clock in my phone lets me know that it's time to get up and get ready to go to work every morning. Why do I have to get up so early? Well, that's because I need to have a big breakfast before I go to work. I have peanut butter and strawberry jam **spread around** toast, cereal with milk, and a banana. Sometimes I have a bowl of rice and hot soup with various side dishes. If I don't fill myself up with enough food, I just cannot **function**. I get **easily agitated** when I'm hungry. I know there are a lot of people out there who would rather **skip** breakfast and get more sleep. They would say a cup of nicely **brewed** hot coffee is all they need for breakfast. I don't want to sound **judgmental**, but I think that is very unhealthy.

Vocabulary

spread around ~에 바르다, 퍼지다
function 기능하다, 역할을 하다, 작동하다
easily agitated 쉽게 짜증이 나는
skip 깡충깡충 뛰다, 거르다, 생략하다
brew 양조하다, (커피, 차를) 끓이다
judgmental 판단의, 비판하는, 남을 재단하는

아침 식사

오전 4시 30분, 내 휴대폰의 알람은 매일 아침 나에게 일어나서 출근 준비할 시간이라고 알려 준다. 왜 이렇게 일찍 일어나느냐고? 음, 그건 난 출근하기 전에 꼭 아침을 거하게 먹어야 하기 때문이다. 난 땅콩 크림과 딸기 잼을 바른 토스트에 우유와 시리얼 그리고 바나나를 먹는다. 가끔 여러 가지 반찬과 함께 밥과 뜨거운 국을 먹기도 한다. 난 충분히 내 배를 채우지 않으면 제대로 활동하질 못한다. 배가 고프면 쉽게 짜증이 나기도 한다. 아침을 먹지 않고 오히려 잠을 더 자는 편이 낫다고 생각하는 사람들이 많다는 건 나도 안다. 또 따뜻한 커피 한 잔이면 아침 식사로 충분하다고 말하는 사람도 있을 것이다. 그들을 비난하고 싶지는 않지만, 내 생각엔 그건 정말 건강에 안 좋은 것 같다.

Sentence Building

spread around ~에 바르다, 퍼지다, 펼쳐지다

There isn't enough jam to spread around the bread.
I like to spread around on my bed when I have a day off.

빵에 골고루 발라 먹을 잼이 부족해.
난 쉬는 날엔 침대에 퍼져 있는 걸 좋아해.

function 기능하다, 역할을 하다, 작동하다

I cannot function if I don't have my coffee in the morning.
Democracy cannot function properly in this environment.

아침에 커피를 안 마시면 난 제 기능을 못해.
이런 환경에서는 민주주의가 제대로 기능할 수 없어.

easily agitated 쉽게 짜증이 나는

My sister is very easily agitated when I talk with her.
I get easily agitated when it's hot.

우리 누나는 나랑 얘기할 때 자꾸 짜증을 내.
더우면 난 쉽게 짜증이 나.

judgment 판단의, 비판하는, 남을 재단하는

**Don't be so judgmental. Try to accept her for what she is.
I'm not being judgmental. I'm just being truthful.**

너무 비판적인 시각으로 보지 마. 그녀를 있는 그대로 받아들이라고.
난 비판적으로 말하는 게 아니야. 단지 진실을 말하고 있는 거지.

Let's talk about today's topic.

1 What do you eat for breakfast?

2 What do you have to have in order to function?

3 What is the perfect breakfast?

Practice Questions

아래의 해석과 같은 의미가 되도록 빈칸을 채워 보세요.

1 There were so many _____ to choose from.
   골라 먹을 반찬들이 정말 많았어.

2 I figured out how to _____ beer at home.
   집에서 맥주를 양조하는 방법을 알아냈어.

3 There isn't enough jam to _____ the bread.
   빵에 골고루 발라 먹을 잼이 부족해.

괄호 안의 어휘를 이용하여 영작해 보세요.

4 아침에 커피를 안 마시면 난 제 기능을 못해. (function)
   _____

5 우리 누나는 나랑 얘기할 때 자꾸 짜증을 내. (easily agitated)
   _____

6 너무 비판적인 시각으로 보지 마. (judgmental)
   _____

Answers

❶ side dishes ❷ brew ❸ spread around ❹ I cannot function if I don't have my coffee in the morning. ❺ My sister is very easily agitated when I talk with her. ❻ Don't be so judgmental.

Vocabulary Builder

빈칸에 들어갈 어휘를 상자 안에서 골라 적어 보세요.

> **side dish**: extra food on the side on smaller plates
>
> **function**: to work or operate properly
>
> **agitated**: annoyed
>
> **brew**: to make beer or coffee or tea by boiling or steeping
>
> **judgmental**: being negative toward a person because of your own reasons

1 I'm too busy to _____ coffee this morning.

2 These days when I talk to my girlfriend, she is very easily _____.

3 Do you like this _____? It's a kind of kimchi.

4 You're such a _____ person for not accepting her.

5 My brain doesn't _____ well when I'm hungry.

Answers
❶ brew ❷ agitated ❸ side dish ❹ judgmental ❺ function

Do you cook?

소리 내어 읽고 해석해 보세요.

I wouldn't call myself a cook, but I've been known to make some pretty good Dduckbokki. How good am I? I don't want to sound like I'm **boasting** or anything, but I've never had any Dduckbokki better than mine. **There, I said it.** Yes, indeed, I am the best Dduckbokki cook in the whole world. **Not only is it delicious, but** I can make it damn quick too. Give me just 10 minutes, I can serve you a dish of Dduckbokki you've never had in your life. I know, I know. I sound **full of myself,** but **save it** until you've tasted my Dduckbokki. I can make other dishes like curry rice, **stir-fried** rice, and spaghetti too. But they are not as good as my Dduckbokki. If you want to try my Dduckbokki, just bring me the **ingredients** and I'll cook for you.

Vocabulary

I wouldn't call myself ~ (자신에 대해서 설명할 때) 나를 ~라고 할 수는 없겠지만, 내가 ~ 정도까지는 아니지만
boast 자랑하다, 뽐내다
There, I said it. 남들이 비판하거나 고깝게 볼 수 있는 말을 소신껏 한 후에 하는 말
not only is it A, but B A일뿐만 아니라, B하기까지 하다
full of oneself 자만한, 스스로에게 도취된
save it (그 이야기는) 그만해
stir-fried (채소·고기 다진 것을 기름을 조금만 넣고 재빨리) 볶은
ingredient (특히 요리 등의) 재료

요리하세요?

요리사 수준까지는 아니지만, 내가 떡볶이만큼은 정말 잘 만든다고 다들 그러네. 얼마나 잘하냐고? 뭐, 좀 너무 잘난 척하는 것 같지만, 난 여태까지 내 떡볶이보다 더 맛있는 떡볶이는 먹어 본 적이 없어. 정말이라니까. 그래, 나는 떡볶이의 대가야. 맛있게 만들 뿐만 아니라 엄청 빨리 만기도 해. 나한테 딱 10분만 줘 봐, 살면서 지금까지 한 번도 맛보지 못한 떡볶이의 신세계를 경험하게 해 줄 테니까. 그래, 나도 알아. 거만이 하늘을 찌르고 있다는 거, 하지만 일단 내 떡볶이를 먹어 보면 알게 될 거야. 난 카레라이스, 볶음밥, 스파게티 같은 것도 만들 줄은 아는데 떡볶이만큼 맛있지는 않아. 내 떡볶이를 한번 맛보고 싶다면, 재료만 가져와, 내가 널 위해 요리해 줄게.

Sentence Building

I wouldn't call myself ~ (자신에 대해서 설명할 때) 나를 ~라고 할 수는 없겠지만, 내가 ~정도까지는 아니지만

I wouldn't call myself an expert, but I am pretty good.
I wouldn't call myself a writer, but I make my living writing online.

전문가까지는 아니지만, 그래도 난 꽤 잘하는 편이지.
작가라고 부르긴 뭐 하지만, 난 인터넷에 글 올리는 일로 먹고살아.

not only is it A, but B A일뿐만 아니라, B하기까지 하다

Not only is it cheap, but it's very delicious.
Not only is it funny, but it's very educational.

가격이 저렴할 뿐만 아니라 아주 맛있어.
웃길 뿐만 아니라 교육적이기까지 해.

full of oneself 자만한, 스스로에게 도취된

God, Jerry is just so full of himself.
I can't believe how full of yourself you are.

이런, 제리는 자뻑이야.
넌 어쩜 그렇게 자아도취에 빠져 있는지 정말 대단하다.

save it (그 이야기는) 그만해

Hey, save it until you see it for yourself.
Save it! I don't want to hear it.

야, 네가 직접 보기 전까지는 아무 말도 하지 마.
그만해! 듣고 싶지 않아.

Let's talk about today's topic.

1   Can you cook? What is your best dish?

2   Do you think cooking for yourself is better than eating out? Why?

3   How often do you go to restaurants?

Practice Questions

아래의 해석과 같은 의미가 되도록 빈칸을 채워 보세요.

1 Don't _____ about your child's talent.
자신의 아이의 재능에 대해서 자랑하지 말아라.

2 My favorite dish is _____ noodles.
내가 제일 좋아하는 음식은 볶음면이야.

3 _____ an expert, but I am pretty good.
전문가까지는 아니지만, 그래도 난 꽤 잘하는 편이지.

괄호 안의 어휘를 이용하여 영작해 보세요.

4 가격이 저렴할 뿐만 아니라 아주 맛있어. (not only is it A, but B)
_____

5 제리는 자뻑이야. (full of oneself)
_____

6 야, 네가 직접 보기 전까지는 아무 말도 하지 마. (save it)
_____

Answers
❶ boast ❷ stir-fried ❸ I wouldn't call myself ❹ Not only is it cheap, but it's very delicious.
❺ Jerry is just so full of himself. ❻ Hey, save it until you see it for yourself.

Vocabulary Builder

빈칸에 들어갈 어휘를 상자 안에서 골라 적어 보세요.

> **boast**: to speak with pride about oneself
>
> **stir-fried**: cooked in a pan
>
> **full of oneself**: thinking too highly of oneself
>
> **save it**: keeping opinions to oneself
>
> **ingredient**: a part of the whole dish

1. One should never be _____ when talking to other people.

2. I love to eat _____ rice when I go to Chinese restaurants.

3. If you think you're right in this situation, just _____ until later.

4. What _____ do you use to make this dish so spicy?

5. I don't like to _____ when I say I'm the best on my soccer team.

Answers
❶ full of oneself ❷ stir-fried ❸ save it ❹ ingredient ❺ boast

Grocery shopping

소리 내어 읽고 해석해 보세요.

Going grocery shopping **back in the day** was a lot easier than now because you had only two choices between a traditional market place and a small supermarket in your neighborhood. Nowadays, we **are bombarded with** a variety of choices like E-mart, Home-plus, Lotte-mart, Costco, etc. It's nice to have many choices but sometimes I **get headaches from** trying to compare all their prices and choose the best one. And another issue is that it becomes very **inconvenient** when small supermarkets near my place **go out of business** because then, I **have no choice but to** go to the big chain stores, which are not **walking distance** from where I live. I miss **the old days**.

Vocabulary

back in the day 옛날에, 예전에
be bombarded with[by] ~로[의해] 폭격을 받다
get headaches from ~로 인해 머리가 아프다
inconvenient (자신의 필요나 바람에 맞지 않아) 불편한, 곤란한
go out of business 파산하다
have no choice but to ~할 수밖에 선택의 여지가 없다
walking distance 걸어갈 수 있는 거리
the old days 예전, 옛날

장보기

예전에는 장 보러 가는 게 요즘보다 훨씬 더 쉬웠는데 그건 선택권이 딱 두 군데, 재래시장 아니면 동네 슈퍼밖에 없었기 때문이지. 요즘엔 이마트, 홈플러스, 롯데마트, 코스트코 등등 너무 고를 때가 많아서 정신이 없을 지경이야. 선택권이 많다는 게 좋기도 하지만 때로는 여기저기 가격 다 비교해 보고 가장 좋은 데를 고르다 보면 머리가 아플 정도라니까. 그리고 또 동네슈퍼는 가까워서 걸어가도 됐는데, 대형마트들 때문에 슈퍼가 망해 버리면 어쩔 수 없이 멀리까지 나가야 해서 불편해. 옛날이 그리워.

Sentence Building

back in the day 옛날에, 예전에

Back in the day, students used to respect their teachers.
Back in the day, we used to get drunk every night.

예전엔 학생들이 선생님들을 공경했었지.
옛날에 우리 매일 밤 술을 엄청 마시곤 했지.

be bombarded with[by] ~로[의해] 폭격을 받다

I hate being bombarded with so many alcohol advertisements.
We are constantly bombarded by the media.

넘쳐 나는 술 광고에 치이는 게 이젠 지겨울 정도다.
우리는 대중매체에 끊임없이 폭격당하고 있다.

get headaches from ~로 인해 머리가 아프다

I get headaches from all the different paint colors to choose from.
I get headaches from reading while I'm on the bus.

페인트 색깔이 너무 많아서 고르는 것만으로도 머리가 아플 지경이야.
버스에서 책을 읽으면 머리가 아프다.

have no choice but to ~할 수밖에 선택의 여지가 없다

I have no choice but to ask you to leave.
I have no choice but to run away.

자네를 해고할 수밖에 달리 선택의 여지가 없네.
난 도망가는 것밖에 선택의 여지가 없어.

Let's talk about today's topic.

1 Which supermarket chain is your favorite to shop at?

2 What do you always have to buy when you go shopping?

3 What is the advantage/disadvantage of shopping at a smaller supermarket?

Practice Questions

아래의 해석과 같은 의미가 되도록 빈칸을 채워 보세요.

1 Often, the truth can be _____.
종종 진실은 불편하기도 해.

2 The museum is within _____ from here.
그 박물관은 여기에서 걸어갈 수 있는 거리에 있어요.

3 _____, we used to get drunk every night.
옛날에 우리 매일 밤 술을 엄청 마시곤 했지.

괄호 안의 어휘를 이용하여 영작해 보세요.

4 넘쳐 나는 술 광고에 치이는 게 이젠 지겨울 정도다. (be bombarded with)

_____

5 버스에서 책을 읽으면 머리가 아프다. (get headaches from)

_____

6 난 도망가는 것밖에 선택의 여지가 없어. (have no choice but to)

_____

Answers
❶ inconvenient ❷ walking distance ❸ Back in the day, ❹ I hate being bombarded with so many alcohol advertisements. ❺ I get headaches from reading while I'm on the bus.
❻ I have no choice but to run away.

Vocabulary Builder

빈칸에 들어갈 어휘를 상자 안에서 골라 적어 보세요.

> **back in the day**: thinking about the times in the past
>
> **bombard**: to attack with a lot of force
>
> **inconvenient**: not good for one's purposes
>
> **go out of business**: close down
>
> **walking distance**: near enough to walk to

1. Things were so much easier _____.

2. It's so _____ that I can't drive to work because of the construction.

3. If we don't get more customers, we'll have to _____.

4. Don't _____ me with a bunch of information I don't understand.

5. Let's go to the bar because it's within _____.

Answers
❶ back in the day ❷ inconvenient ❸ go out of business ❹ bombard ❺ walking distance

Food shows on TV

소리 내어 읽고 해석해 보세요.

Tasty Road, Olive Show, Master Chef Korea, **you name it**, there are just so many food or cooking shows, which in Korean is called "Muk-bang" on TV these days. It's quite a **phenomenon**. I don't know how long this trend is going to last, but they seem to **sell really well**. The viewers love it, so why not put more shows on when it's a hot genre? Do I enjoy those shows? Not really. But I hear a lot of guys who have never cooked in their lives started cooking, and their wives love it. And cookware sales **are heating up like never before**. **The economy is taking off** and spending is growing and girls are happy, **what more can you ask for?**

Vocabulary

you name it (이것저것 사물의 보기를 열거한 뒤) 그 밖에 무엇이든지, 전부, 무엇이든지 말해 봐요
phenomenon 현상
sell really well (매우) 잘 팔리다
be heating up like never before 그 어느 때보다 달아오르고[뜨거워지고] 있다
take off 급격히 인기를 얻다, 뜨다, 날아오르다, 활기를 띄게 되다
the economy is taking off 경제[경기]가 살아나고 있다
What more can you ask for? 더 이상 무엇을 바라겠는가?

TV 먹방

〈테이스티 로드〉, 〈올리브 쇼〉, 〈마스터 셰프 코리아〉, 이름을 다 대기도 힘들 정도로 요즘에는 TV만 켜면 한국어로 일명 '먹방(먹는 방송)'이라 불리는 음식·요리 쇼가 정말 많다. 정말 놀라운 일이지. 이런 현상이 언제까지 계속될지는 모르지만, 지금으로써는 이런 프로그램들이 대세인 것만은 인정. 시청자들이 좋아하는데, 방송사 입장에서야 계속 더 만들지 않을 이유가 없지 않겠어? 나도 이런 방송을 좋아하냐고? 별로. 그런데 요즘 평생 요리 한 번 안 해 본 남자들이 요리를 하기 시작하니까 아내들이 엄청 좋아한다더라고. 게다가 주방 제품이 그 어느 때보다도 날개 돋친 듯 팔리고 있다네. 경기도 살아나고 소비도 늘고 여자들도 행복해지니, 더 이상 뭘 더 바라겠어?

Sentence Building

you name it (이것저것 사물의 보기를 열거한 뒤) 그 밖에 무엇이든지, 전부, 무엇이든지 말해 봐요

You name it, I'll do it for you.
I am willing to talk about anything - politics, religion, philosophy, you name it.

무엇이든 말만 해요, 내가 해드릴 테니.
난 무엇에 관해서든 대화할 의향이 있어, 정치, 종교, 철학, 뭐든 말만해.

be heating up like never before
그 어느 때보다 달아오르고[뜨거워지고] 있다

When the celebrity started using the lipstick, sales were heating up like never before.
Competition is heating up like never before.

그 연예인이 그 립스틱을 사용하기 시작하고 나서는 전에 없이 판매량이 늘었어.
경쟁이 그 어느 때보다 과열되고 있군.

the economy is taking off 경제[경기]가 살아나고 있다

The economy is taking off and people are buying big ticket items.
It's a sign that the economy is taking off.

경제가 살아나면서 사람들이 고가의 물건들을 많이 사고 있어.
경기가 다시 살아나고 있다는 신호야.

What more can you ask for? 더 이상 무엇을 바라겠는가?

It's delicious and cheap? What more can you ask for?
Good food, friends, and music. What more can you ask for?

맛도 있고 싸다고? 그 이상 뭘 더 바라겠어?
맛있는 음식, 친구들, 그리고 음악까지. 더 이상 무엇을 바라겠는가?

# Let's talk about today's topic.

1. Do you watch cooking or food shows? Which one is your favorite?

2. Why do you think these cooking/food shows are so popular these days?

3. Have you ever been to the restaurants they show on TV shows?

Practice Questions

아래의 해석과 같은 의미가 되도록 빈칸을 채워 보세요.

1 Have you ever experienced a paranormal _____?
초자연적 현상을 경험해 본 적이 있나요?

2 You cannot please all the _____ all the time.
모든 시청자들을 늘 만족시킬 수는 없어.

3 _____, I'll do it for you.
무엇이든 말만 해요, 내가 해드릴 테니.

괄호 안의 어휘를 이용하여 영작해 보세요.

4 경쟁이 그 어느 때보다 과열되고 있군. (be heating up like never before)

_____

5 경제가 살아나면서 사람들이 고가의 물건들을 많이 사고 있어.
(the economy is taking off)

_____

6 맛도 있고 싸다고? 그 이상 뭘 더 바라겠어?
(what more can you ask for?)

_____

Answers
❶ phenomenon ❷ viewers ❸ You name it, ❹ Competition is heating up like never before.
❺ The economy is taking off and people are buying big ticket items. ❻ It's delicious and cheap? What more can you ask for?

Vocabulary Builder

빈칸에 들어갈 어휘를 상자 안에서 골라 적어 보세요.

> **you name it**: anything, anything you say or choose
>
> **phenomenon**: an unbelievable fact that can be seen
>
> **viewer**: somebody who watches something
>
> **heat up**: to become popular
>
> **take off**: to increase rapidly

1 When the economy _____, it's good for businesses.

2 The foreign language learning _____ has died out in recent years.

3 Audi, BMW, Mercedes, Porsche, _____, we have everything.

4 I'm an avid "Reply 1988" _____.

5 Watch and see if this new brand of cologne will _____.

Answers
❶ takes off ❷ phenomenon ❸ you name it ❹ viewer ❺ heat up

School uniforms

소리 내어 읽고 해석해 보세요.

Should students have to wear school uniforms? Personally, I think wearing school uniforms can bring **a sense of unity** among students and also help them **relive** memories when they **look back on** the **school days**. On the other hand, **one may argue** that it destroys **individuality** and freedom. I know this is a **hot-button topic**, so I should be really careful when I give my opinion on this. So, I won't say anymore. By the way, I see some high school girls make their uniform skirts so short these days, is that even legal? I understand how they want to look more **appealing** and cool but I wonder what their parents or teachers say about that.

Vocabulary

a sense of unity 일체감, 동질감
relive 예전의 기억이나 과거에 체험했던 것을 (특히 상상 속에서) 다시 체험하다
look back on ~을 뒤돌아보다
school days 학창시절
one may argue ~라고 주장하는 사람도 있다, ~라고 주장할 수도 있다
individuality 개성, 특성
hot-button topic[issue] 뜨거운 주제[쟁점]
appealing 매력적인, 흥미로운

교복

학생들이 꼭 교복을 입어야만 할까? 개인적인 생각으로는, 교복을 입으면 학생들이 일체감을 느낄 수 있고 나중에 학창 시절을 되돌아볼 때 좋은 추억들도 떠오를 것 같은데 말이야. 다른 한편으로는, 학생들의 개성과 자유가 침해당한다고 볼 수도 있겠지. 교복 문제가 워낙 뜨거운 논란거리라서 의견을 말하기가 정말 조심스러워. 그러니까 더는 얘기 안 할래. 그런데, 요즘 교복 치마를 엄청 짧게 입고 다니는 여학생들이 있던데, 그건 괜찮은 건가? 물론 여학생들이 더 예쁘고 매력적으로 보이고 싶어서 그런 건 알겠지만 그들의 부모님들이나 선생님들은 어떻게 생각할지 참 궁금하네.

Sentence Building

a sense of unity 일체감, 동질감

Religions promote a sense of unity. I feel a sense of unity with those that think the same as I.

종교는 일체감을 고취시키지.
나와 같은 생각을 하는 사람들과 난 동질감을 느낀다.

look back on 되돌아보다, 회상하다

When I look back on my life, I regret nothing.
When I look back on my college life, it brings back so many memories.

내 인생을 되돌아볼 때 난 전혀 후회가 없어.
대학 시절을 회상하면 정말 많은 추억들이 떠올라.

one may argue ~라고 주장하는 사람도 있다, ~라고 주장할 수도 있다

One may argue that apples are better than pears, but I won't.
One may argue that marriage is only a contract.

사과가 배보다 낫다고 주장하는 사람들도 있지만, 난 그렇게 생각하지 않는다.
어떤 사람들은 결혼은 그냥 계약일 뿐이라고 주장하기도 한다.

hot-button topic[issue] 뜨거운 주제[쟁점]

Politics is a very hot-button topic.
Privacy is a hot-button issue these days.

정치 이야기는 아주 뜨거운 주제지.
사생활 문제는 요즘 뜨거운 쟁점이야.

Let's talk about today's topic.

1. What do you think about school uniforms?
   (The pros and cons of school uniforms)

2. Does wearing a school uniform improve student behavior?

3. Should school uniform skirts be a certain length?

Practice Questions

아래의 해석과 같은 의미가 되도록 빈칸을 채워 보세요.

1 I miss my _____.
학창 시절이 그리워.

2 The programs looked very _____ to me.
그 프로그램들은 나에게 매우 매력적으로 보였다.

3 Religions promote a _____.
종교는 일체감을 고취시키지.

괄호 안의 어휘를 이용하여 영작해 보세요.

4 내 인생을 되돌아볼 때 난 전혀 후회가 없어. (look back on)
_____

5 어떤 사람들은 결혼은 그냥 계약일 뿐이라고 주장하기도 한다.
(one may argue)
_____

6 정치 이야기는 아주 뜨거운 주제지. (hot-button topic)
_____

Answers
❶ school days ❷ appealing ❸ sense of unity ❹ When I look back on my life, I regret nothing. ❺ One may argue that marriage is only a contract. ❻ Politics is a very hot-button topic.

Vocabulary Builder

빈칸에 들어갈 어휘를 상자 안에서 골라 적어 보세요.

> **sense of unity**: feeling together with others
>
> **look back on**: reflect about the past
>
> **individuality**: being unique in one's own way
>
> **hot-button**: controversial or popular topic
>
> **appealing**: seeming to be good

1. If I wear this silly hat, I feel like I have my own _____.

2. When I _____ my school days, I miss many of my friends.

3. Traveling abroad is very _____.

4. I feel a _____ when I'm with my good friends.

5. I don't like to talk about _____ issues.

Answers
❶ individuality ❷ look back on ❸ appealing ❹ sense of unity ❺ hot-button

Study groups

소리 내어 읽고 해석해 보세요.

Pamela Where **are** you **headed**?

Roy I'm going to English study group.

Pamela Oh, I didn't know you went to study group meetings. How long have you been doing this?

Roy We just started last week. This is our second meeting.

Pamela How was the first meeting? Do you think **it helps**?

Roy It was great. They are all very friendly and **enthusiastic** about studying English. I think it's a lot better than studying by myself.

Pamela **Awesome**!

Roy You want to join us? You'd be **more than welcome** to join us.

Pamela I think **I'll pass**. If I come, the guys in your group won't be able to concentrate on studying. You know how guys always **fall for me**.

Roy **Get real**, Pam!

Vocabulary

be headed (for) ~로 향하다
it helps 도움이 되다
enthusiastic 열정적인
awesome 어마어마한, 기막힌, 멋진
more than welcome 더 없이 환영하는 (welcome의 강조 표현)
I'll pass 난 안 할래
fall for someone[something] ~을 좋아하다, ~에 빠지다, ~에 넘어가다
get real 현실을 직시해, 꿈 깨, 정신 차려, 진지하게 바라보다

스터디 모임

Pamela 어디에 가?

Roy 영어 스터디 모임에 가는 중이야.

Pamela 어, 네가 스터디 모임에 다니는지 몰랐어. 언제부터 한 거야?

Roy 지난주에 막 시작했어. 이번이 두 번째 모임이야.

Pamela 첫 모임은 어땠어? 도움이 되는 것 같아?

Roy 아주 좋더라고. 다들 친절하고 영어공부에 대한 열정도 대단해. 혼자 공부하는 것보다 훨씬 나은 것 같아.

Pamela 좋네!

Roy 너도 같이할래? 너 오면 모두 좋아할 거야.

Pamela 난 안 할래. 내가 가면 모임에 있는 남자애들이 공부에 집중을 못 할 거야. 너도 알다시피 남자애들이 나만 보면 사족을 못 쓰잖니.

Roy 정신 차려, 팸!

Sentence Building

more than welcome 더 없이 환영하는 (welcome의 강조 표현)

You're more than welcome to join me at this table.
You are more than welcome to be here.

우리 테이블에 같이 앉는 거 대환영이야.
여기에 온 것 두 팔 벌려 환영해.

I'll pass 난 안 할래

Go to the mall? I'll pass.
I'll pass on the coffee because I'm in a hurry.

쇼핑몰에 가자고? 난 안 갈래.
전 커피 안 마실게요, 급히 볼일이 있어서요.

fall for something[someone]
~을 좋아하다, ~에 빠지다, ~에 넘어가다

I'm not going to fall for that prank again.
How can you fall for her? She's a bitch.

그런 장난에 다시는 안 넘어갈 거야.
어떻게 그 여자에게 빠질 수가 있니? 걔 아주 못된 애야.

get real 현실을 직시해, 꿈 깨, 정신 차려, 진지하게 바라보다

Get real, Suzy is way hotter than Hyeri.
You need to get real about your weaknesses.

왜 이러니 진짜, 수지가 헤리보다 훨씬 예뻐.
네 약점들을 직시해야 해.

Let's talk about today's topic.

1 What has been your experience with study groups?

2 How do you study in study groups?

3 Are study groups helpful to learn?

Practice Questions

아래의 해석과 같은 의미가 되도록 빈칸을 채워 보세요.

1 Where are you _____?
  어디에 가니? (어디로 향하고 있니?)

2 There were really _____ about the idea.
  그들은 그 아이디어에 대해 정말 열광했다.

3 You are _____ to be here.
  여기에 온 것 두 팔 벌려 환영해.

괄호 안의 어휘를 이용하여 영작해 보세요.

4 쇼핑몰에 가자고? 난 안 갈래. (I'll pass)
  _____

5 그런 장난에 다시는 안 넘어갈 거야. (fall for something)
  _____

6 왜 이러니 진짜, 수지가 혜리보다 훨씬 예뻐. (get real)
  _____

Answers
❶ headed ❷ enthusiastic ❸ more than welcome ❹ Go to the mall? I'll pass. ❺ I'm not going to fall for that prank again. ❻ Get real, Suzy is way hotter than Hyeri.

Vocabulary Builder

빈칸에 들어갈 어휘를 상자 안에서 골라 적어 보세요.

> **head**: to move in a particular direction
>
> **enthusiastic**: excited
>
> **more than welcome**: very welcome
>
> **fall for someone**: suddenly love someone
>
> **get real**: to see the reality

1 I'm going to _____ to the store. Want to join?

2 He's _____ to come with us if he wants.

3 I am not _____ about anything.

4 It's time for Betty to wake up and _____.

5 Tom is such a romantic it's easy for him to

_____.

Answers
❶ head ❷ more than welcome ❸ enthusiastic ❹ get real ❺ fall for someone

Social clubs

소리 내어 읽고 해석해 보세요.

Arthur Mia, have you ever joined a social club before?

Mia I joined a golf **social club** once, but I quit after the first meeting.

Arthur Why?

Mia I was the only female in the group **out of 20 people**.

Arthur Haha. That must have been really **awkward**.

Mia **Tell me about it!** How about you? Are you in any social clubs?

Arthur Yes, I am. I'm in Sunday morning soccer club, wine **tasters** club, social dance club, and a club where all the members have the same **Zodiac sign**.

Mia Oh my god! How can you **find time to do** all that? And what's that club you just mentioned? A club where people have the same Zodiac sign?

Arthur It's a club for those who have the same Zodiac sign.

Mia **Give me a break!**

Vocabulary

social club 사교 모임
out of + 숫자 몇 명[개] 중에
awkward 어색한
tell me about it 그러게 말이야, 내 말이, (나도 겪어 봐서) 무슨 말인지 잘 안다
taster 맛 감식가, 감별사
Zodiac sign 별자리
find time to ~ ~할 시간을 내다, ~할 틈을 내다
Give me a break! (상대방이 한 말이나 행동에 동조하기 어려울 때)
(말도 안 되는 소리) 그만 좀 해! / 적당히 좀 해!

동호회

Arthur 미아야, 너 동호회 모임에 가 본 적 있어?
Mia 골프 동호회에 한 번 가 봤는데, 첫 모임 후에 탈퇴했어.
Arthur 왜?
Mia 20명이 모였는데 나만 여자더라고.
Arthur 하하. 진짜 어색했겠네.
Mia 말도 마! 넌? 참석하는 동호회 있어?
Arthur 응. 난 일요 조기 축구, 와인 테이스팅, 사교댄스, 그리고 같은 별자리 동호회에 나가.
Mia 맙소사! 그걸 다 할 시간이 있어? 그런데 방금 말한 그 동호회는 뭐야? 같은 별자리 동호회?
Arthur 별자리가 같은 사람들이 모이는 동호회야.
Mia 아이고, 제발!

Sentence Building

out of + 숫자 몇 명[개] 중에

Out of 40 students, I was the only one that got an A!
Only 2 out of 10 applicants are female.

40명 학생 중 A학점을 받은 사람은 나밖에 없었어!
신청자 10명 중 2명만 여자였어.

Tell me about it! 그러게 말이야, 내 말이

Tell me about it! I can't stand him, either.
Tell me about it! This winter has been ridiculously cold.

내 말이! 나도 걔는 정말 짜증나서 못 견디겠어.
그러게 말이야! 이번 겨울은 말도 안 되게 춥네.

find time to ~ ~할 시간을 내다, ~할 틈을 내다

It's hard to find time to study when all these activities are going on.
I couldn't find time to work out because I was so busy.

이렇게 활동이 많으면 공부할 시간을 내기가 어려워요.
너무 바빠서 운동하러 갈 시간을 낼 수가 없었어.

Give me a break! (상대방이 한 말이나 행동에 동조하기 어려울 때)
(말도 안 되는 소리) 그만 좀 해! / 적당히 좀 해!

Give me a break! Jess is so not interested in Blake.
Give me a break! You can't possibly be that stupid.

말도 안 되는 소리 그만해! 제스는 블레이크한테 전혀 관심 없어.
이러지 좀 마! 네가 설마 그렇게까지 무식하진 않겠지.

Let's talk about today's topic.

1 What clubs have you ever been a part of?

2 Are there some clubs you are interested in?

3 Are there clubs that seem awkward or weird for existing?

Practice Questions

아래의 해석과 같은 의미가 되도록 빈칸을 채워 보세요.

1 There was an _____ silence.
어색한 정적이 흘렀다.

2 We have the same _____.
우린 별자리가 같아.

3 _____, I was the only one that got an A!
40명의 학생 중 A학점을 받은 사람은 나밖에 없었어!

괄호 안의 어휘를 이용하여 영작해 보세요.

4 그러게 말이야. 이번 겨울은 말도 안 되게 춥네. (tell me about it)

_____

5 너무 바빠서 운동하러 갈 시간을 낼 수가 없었어. (find time to ~)

_____

6 말도 안 되는 소리 그만해! 제스는 블레이크한테 전혀 관심 없어.
(give me a break)

_____

Answers

❶ awkward ❷ Zodiac sign ❸ Out of 40 students ❹ Tell me about it. This winter has been ridiculously cold. ❺ I couldn't find time to work out because I was so busy. ❻ Give me a break! Jess is so not interested in Blake.

Vocabulary Builder

빈칸에 들어갈 어휘를 상자 안에서 골라 적어 보세요.

> **out of**: from among an amount or number
>
> **awkward**: strange or weird
>
> **Tell me about it!**: I totally understand
>
> **Zodiac sign**: astrological sign based on your birth month
>
> **Give me a break!**: I don't believe you

1 Jim is such an _____ guy. He doesn't talk to anyone.

2 _____! I think Jenny is a hottie too!

3 $5 for an Americano? _____!

4 _____ 10 days, 5 are being spent in the Philippines.

5 My _____ is Aries.

Answers
❶ awkward ❷ tell me about it ❸ give me a break ❹ out of ❺ Zodiac sign

Unit 21　**Do you share any chores around your house?**
　　　　집안일을 분담해서 하나요?
Unit 22　**Noise between apartment floors**
　　　　층간 소음
Unit 23　**Sexual harassment**
　　　　성추행
Unit 24　**Online shopping**
　　　　온라인 쇼핑
Unit 25　**Buying directly from sites abroad**
　　　　해외 직구
Unit 26　**Do you have a religion?**
　　　　종교가 있나요?
Unit 27　**Podcasts**
　　　　팟캐스트
Unit 28　**Fitness craze**
　　　　몸짱 열풍
Unit 29　**Tattoos**
　　　　문신
Unit 30　**Fortune-telling**
　　　　점

Part 3

Do you share any chores around your house?

소리 내어 읽고 해석해 보세요.

For the past 60 years or so, my dad has never done any **housework**, but left everything to my mom. For our parents' generation, I guess **that's just how it worked** for most of the family in Korea. But recently he started **doing dishes** and **laundry** and taking garbage out to the **dumpster**, and even going grocery shopping with my mom. **Like they say, times have changed.** Today, husbands do share the housework with their wives **a whole lot** more than before, perhaps not as much as their wives want them to, but still more and more guys are doing **their share of work**. How much should a husband participate in housework? Well, I guess that's something every family has to decide **on their own**.

Vocabulary

housework 가사, 집안일
that's just how it works 원래 그런 거야, 원래 이런 식으로 작동해
do (the) dishes 설거지를 하다
laundry 세탁, 세탁물
dumpster 대형 쓰레기 수거 용기
like they say 사람들이 말하듯이, 흔히 말하듯이
times have changed 시대가 변했다
a whole lot 아주 많은, a lot의 강조형
one's share of work ~의 몫의 일
on one's own 혼자서, 자력으로, 단독으로

집안일을 분담해서 하나요?

지난 60여 년간 우리 아빠는 집안일을 모두 엄마에게 맡기고 단 한 번도 한 적이 없다. 우리 부모님 세대의 대부분 한국 가정에서는 그런 식으로 지낸 것 같긴 해. 그런데 요즘엔 우리 아빠가 설거지도 하고 빨래도 하고 쓰레기도 내다 버리고 심지어는 엄마와 장을 보러 가기까지 하셔. 흔히 말하듯 시대가 변한 거겠지. 요즘 시대의 남편들은 정말 예전보다 많이 집안일을 아내와 분담해서 하고 있어. 물론 아내들이 원하는 만큼은 아니겠지만, 그래도 계속해서 더 많은 남자가 자신이 해야 할 몫을 하고 있어. 과연 남편들은 어느 정도 집안일에 참여해야 하는 걸까? 흠, 그건 뭐 각 가정이 알아서 결정할 일인 것 같네.

Sentence Building

that's just how it works
원래 그런 거야, 원래 이런 식으로 작동해

Don't question it. That's just how it works.
Push the button. That's just how this thing works.

묻지 마. 원래 그런 거야.
버튼을 눌러. 그건 원래 그렇게 작동하는 거야.

like they say 사람들이 말하듯이, 흔히 말하듯이

Like they say, you are what you eat.
Like they say, bigger is always better.

흔히들 말하는 것처럼, 네가 먹는 음식이 너인 거야. (식습관이 사람을 만들지.)
사람들이 말하듯이, 항상 클수록 더 좋은 거야.

times have changed 시대가 변했다

Times have changed so we need to change with them.
Boy, how times sure have changed!

시대가 변했으니 우리도 그에 발맞춰 변해야 해.
아, 정말 시대가 많이 변하긴 했구나!

one's share of work ~의 몫의 일

You do your share and I'll do my share of the work.
Why does Bobby get a smaller share of the work than I do?

넌 너의 몫을 하고 난 나의 몫의 일을 할게.
왜 바비는 나보다 적은 몫을 담당하는 거야?

Let's talk about today's topic.

1 Do you help out with any of the housework?

2 What chores do you absolutely hate doing?

3 What housework is necessary for you to live?

Practice Questions

아래의 해석과 같은 의미가 되도록 빈칸을 채워 보세요.

1 I have _____ of money.
   난 돈이 아주 많아.

2 You have to do it _____.
   넌 이걸 혼자 힘으로 해야만 해.

3 Don't question it. That's _____.
   묻지 마. 원래 그런 거야.

괄호 안의 어휘를 이용하여 영작해 보세요.

4 사람들이 말하듯이, 항상 클수록 더 좋은 거야. (like they say)
   _____

5 시대가 변했으니 우리도 그에 발맞춰 변해야 해. (times have changed)
   _____

6 넌 너의 몫을 하고 난 나의 몫의 일을 할게. (one's share of work)
   _____

Answers
❶ a whole lot ❷ on your own ❸ just how it works ❹ Like they say, bigger is always better.
❺ Times have changed so we need to change with them. ❻ You do your share and I'll do my share of the work.

Vocabulary Builder

빈칸에 들어갈 어휘를 상자 안에서 골라 적어 보세요.

> **housework**: work to keep your house clean
>
> **do dishes**: washing and putting away dishes
>
> **laundry**: cleaning one's clothes
>
> **grocery shopping**: going out and buying food
>
> **on one's own**: do by one's self

1. I can't go out. I have to wait for the _____ to finish.

2. Look at how empty the fridge is! We have to go _____.

3. This place is so messy I'll be doing _____ forever!

4. Don't worry about me. I can do it _____.

5. Now that dinner is finished, time for you to _____.

Answers
❶ laundry ❷ grocery shopping ❸ housework ❹ on my own ❺ do dishes

139

Unit 22 Noise between apartment floors

소리 내어 읽고 해석해 보세요.

Owen   You live in an apartment, right?

Cindy   Yes, I do. Why?

Owen   Do you ever **run into a problem** with the people **living on the floor above you**?

Cindy   Every single day. The kids upstairs won't stop running around all day.

Owen   What do you do about that?

Cindy   **One time**, I went up and politely asked their mom if they could try to be careful and make less noise. You know what she told me?

Owen   What?

Cindy   She told me that my TV is too loud so she can't go to sleep at night.

Owen   **Right back at you,** huh? So, what did you do?

Cindy   I told her I'm going to call the police if this **keeps happening**. But nothing changed **afterward**.

Owen   What kind of world are we living in!

Vocabulary

run into a problem 문제가 생기다, 문제에 직면하다
live on the floor above someone ~의 위층에 살다
one time 한번은, 예전에
right back at ~에게 바로 반격하다, 받은 대로 바로 돌려주다 (상대방의 인사, 칭찬, 욕 등에 대해서 똑같이 돌려줄 때 우리가 어렸을 때 쓰던 '반사!'라는 말과 비슷한 표현)
keep happening 계속해서 일어나다[발생하다]
afterward 그 후에, 나중에

층간 소음

Owen   너 아파트에 살지, 맞지?

Cindy   응. 왜?

Owen   너희 위층에 사는 사람들하고 문제 생긴 적 없어?

Cindy   매일매일 있지. 윗집 애들이 온종일 집에서 뛰어다녀.

Owen   그래서 어떻게 했어?

Cindy   한번은, 내가 윗집으로 올라가서 걔네들 엄마한테 정중하게 좀만 더 조심해 달라고 조용히 해 달라고 부탁했지. 그런데 나한테 뭐라는 줄 알아?

Owen   뭐라고 했는데?

Cindy   내가 TV를 너무 크게 틀어 놔서 밤에 잠을 못 자겠다는 거야.

Owen   오호라, 바로 반격해 오는데? 그래서, 넌 뭐라고 했어?

Cindy   이런 일이 계속된다면 경찰을 부를 거라고 말했지. 하지만 그 후로도 변한 건 아무것도 없어.

Owen   정말 요지경이다!

Sentence Building

run into a problem 문제가 생기다, 문제에 직면하다

Have you run into any problems with your new boss?
I've run into a problem that I don't know how to solve.

새로 온 직장 상사와 문제 생긴 적 있어?
난 어떻게 해결해야 할지 모를 문제에 직면했다.

one time 한번은, 예전에

One time, I caught a fish this big!
One time, I drank a whole bottle of tequila without eating.

한번은, 내가 엄청 큰 물고기를 잡았었어!
예전에, 안주 없이 데킬라 한병을 다 마신 적이 있어.

right back at ~에게 바로 반격하다, 받은 대로 바로 돌려주다
(상대방의 인사, 칭찬, 욕 등에 대해서 똑같이 돌려줄 때 우리가 어렸을 때 쓰던 '반사!'라는 말과 비슷한 표현)

May snapped right back at him.
Right back at you, bro!

메이는 곧바로 반격에 나서 그에게 쏘아붙였다.
반사, 자식아!

keep happening 계속해서 일어나다[발생하다]

If this keeps happening, I swear we'll break up!
A weird noise keeps happening to this computer.

계속 이러면, 우리 헤어지는 줄 알아!
이 컴퓨터에서 이상한 소리가 계속 나고 있어.

Let's talk about today's topic.

1. What kind of accommodation do you live in? Have you had any problems with your neighbors?

2. If someone living above you kept making an unreasonable amount of noise, how would you resolve the problem?

3. Where would you never want to live? Or where would you like to live?

Practice Questions

아래의 해석과 같은 의미가 되도록 빈칸을 채워 보세요.

1 She calls me _____ day.
그녀는 나에게 매일매일 전화한다.

2 I'm going to _____.
나 경찰 부를 거야.

3 I've _____ that I don't know how to solve.
난 어떻게 해결해야 할지 모를 문제에 직면했다.

괄호 안의 어휘를 이용하여 영작해 보세요.

4 한번은, 내가 엄청 큰 물고기를 잡았었어. (one time)
_____

5 메이는 곧바로 반격에 나서 그에게 쏘아붙였다. (right back at)
_____

6 계속 이러면, 우리 헤어지는 줄 알아! (keep happening)
_____

Answers
❶ every single ❷ call the police ❸ run into a problem ❹ One time, I caught a fish this big.
❺ May snapped right back at him. ❻ If this keeps happening, I swear we'll break up.

Vocabulary Builder

빈칸에 들어갈 어휘를 상자 안에서 골라 적어 보세요.

> **run into**: to encounter unexpectedly
>
> **every single + 명사**: every time, without question
>
> **right back at someone**: turning the conversation to the other person
>
> **afterward**: later time

1. I was having an argument with Rich and he came _____.

2. Have you ever _____ your ex-girlfriend?

3. We fought. But nothing got better _____.

4. _____ he calls late, I feel like he's cheating.

Answers
❶ right back at me ❷ run into ❸ afterward ❹ Every single time

Sexual harassment

소리 내어 읽고 해석해 보세요.

Adam   I was on the subway today and this one girl **accused me of sexual harassment**.

Rosa   What? Why would she think that?

Adam   She thought I was **groping** her.

Rosa   Well, did you?

Adam   Absolutely not! The train was so **packed** and she **was literally pressed up against** me, so it must have been my bag that touched her.

Rosa   Yeah, I can see why she thought that you were touching her. So, what happened then?

Adam   She just **gave me a dirty look** and left saying some **swear words**.

Rosa   **Thank god she didn't call** the police. **It could have been a lot worse**.

Adam   I know. **What a relief!**

Vocabulary

accused A of B A를 B로 비난하다
sexual harassment 성희롱, 성추행
grope (손으로) 더듬다, 몸을 더듬다
packed 가득 찬, 꽉 들어찬
be pressed up against ~와 밀착된, 눌려진
literally (강조 부사) 말 그대로, 문자 그대로
give someone a dirty look 째려보다, 기분 나쁘게 쳐다보다
swear word 욕
thank god + 주어 + 동사 ~해서 다행이다[천만다행이다]
it could have been a lot worse 훨씬 더 심각한 상황이 될 수도 있었다, 큰일 날 뻔했다
What a relief! 정말 다행이야! / 십년감수했네!

성추행

Adam   오늘 지하철에서 어떤 여자가 내가 자기를 성추행했다고 난리 쳤어.

Rosa   뭐? 왜 그 여자가 그렇게 생각한 건데?

Adam   내가 자기 몸을 더듬었다나 뭐라나.

Rosa   헉, 너 진짜 그랬어?

Adam   절대 아니지! 지하철에 사람이 하도 많아서 그 여자가 나한테 완전 딱 붙어 있으니까, 아마 내 가방에 몸이 눌린 거겠지.

Rosa   그래, 그 여자가 오해할 만도 하네. 그래서, 결국 어떻게 됐어?

Adam   그 여자가 나를 막 째려보고 욕하면서 가더라고.

Rosa   그래도 경찰 안 불러서 다행이네. 큰일 날 뻔했다.

Adam   그러게 말이야. 십년감수했어!

Sentence Building

be pressed up against ~에 밀착된, ~에 밀착되어 눌린

Dude, back off. Your bag is pressed up against my crotch.
I can't breathe! I'm pressed up against this rock!

야, 좀 떨어져. 네 가방이 내 가랑이에 눌렸잖아.
숨 막혀! 이 바위가 날 짓누르고 있어!

give someone a dirty look 째려보다, 기분 나쁘게 쳐다보다

I accidentally bumped into Joe and he gave me a dirty look.
I gave her a dirty look when she shushed me.

조와 우연히 부딪쳤는데 그가 나를 기분 나쁘게 쳐다봤어.
그녀가 나에게 '쉿' 조용히 하라고 해서 내가 째려봤어.

thank god + 주어 + 동사 ~해서 다행이다[천만다행이다]

Thank god my sister didn't rat me out to my parents.
Thank god Jenny was there to bail me out.

내 여동생이 부모님한테 고자질 안 해서 정말 다행이야.
제니가 나를 곤경에서 구해 줘서 천만다행이었어.

it could have been a lot worse
훨씬 더 심각한 상황이 될 수도 있었다, 큰일 날 뻔했다

Good thing you got help. It could have been a lot worse.
It could have been a lot worse if you hadn't done it so promptly.

도움을 받아서 정말 다행이구나. 큰일 날 뻔했어.
네가 즉각적으로 대응하지 않았다면 훨씬 더 심각한 상황이 될 수도 있었어.

Let's talk about today's topic.

1. Have you seen anyone sexually harassed in public?

2. Have you ever been accused of something you didn't do?

3. In your opinion, what is the best way to handle conflict with others?

Practice Questions

아래의 해석과 같은 의미가 되도록 빈칸을 채워 보세요.

1 The bar is _____.
술집에 사람들이 꽉 들어찼다.

2 What _____!
십년감수했네!

3 Dude, back off. Your bag is _____ my crotch.
야, 좀 떨어져. 네 가방이 내 가랑이에 눌렸잖아.

괄호 안의 어휘를 이용하여 영작해 보세요.

4 그녀가 나에게 '쉿' 조용히 하라고 해서 내가 째려봤어.
(give someone a dirty look)

_____

5 제니가 나를 곤경에서 구해 줘서 천만다행이었어.
(thank god + 주어 + 동사)

_____

6 네가 즉각적으로 대응하지 않았다면 훨씬 더 심각한 상황이 될 수도 있었어.
(it could have been a lot worse)

_____

Answers
❶ packed ❷ a relief ❸ pressed up against ❹ I gave her a dirty look when she shushed me.
❺ Thank god Jenny was there to bail me out. ❻ It could have been a lot worse if you hadn't done it so promptly.

Vocabulary Builder

빈칸에 들어갈 어휘를 상자 안에서 골라 적어 보세요.

> **sexual harassment**: unwanted sexual contact or words from others
>
> **grope**: feel something heavily with the hands
>
> **swear word**: a bad word or curse
>
> **What a relief!**: Thank god!

1. I made the baseball team. _____!

2. Be quiet! You can't say a _____ in a church!

3. Jerry's in trouble. He got written up for _____.

4. When I'm on a packed subway, I feel like I'm being _____.

Answers
❶ What a relief ❷ swear word ❸ sexual harassment ❹ groped

Online shopping

소리 내어 읽고 해석해 보세요.

Eve   Do you **prefer to** shop in a store or online?

Shawn Definitely online. Everything is a lot cheaper online. What about you?

Eve   **I do a little bit of both**. I mean, like, I usually go to the store to **check out the real product first** and compare it with the online price, then buy it from where it's cheaper.

Shawn Wow, very smart! **Why didn't I think of that?**

Eve   Probably because you are too lazy?

Shawn Hey, how did you know I was lazy? You are very **intuitive**. Anyways, I guess another reason I shop online is because I like **having things delivered to** my door. I feel like I'm getting a present from someone.

Eve   That's an interesting **point of view**.

Vocabulary

prefer to ~하는 게 더 좋다
a little bit of both 두 가지 다 조금씩
check something out first ~을 먼저 확인해[봐] 두다
Why didn't I think of that? 난 왜 그 생각을 못 했을까?
intuitive 직관[직감]에 의한, 직관력이 있는
have something delivered to ~ ~로 배송받다
point of view 관점, 견해

온라인 쇼핑

Eve 넌 가게에 가서 물건을 사는 게 더 좋아, 아니면 온라인에서 사는 게 더 좋아?

Shawn 당연히 온라인에서지. 온라인으로 사야 뭐든지 더 싸잖아. 넌?

Eve 난 둘 다 조금씩 해. 그러니까 내 말은, 난 가게에 가서 실제 물건을 먼저 보고 온라인 가격이랑 비교한 다음에 더 싼 걸로 사.

Shawn 와, 정말 똑똑한데! 난 왜 그 생각을 못 했지?

Eve 아마도 네가 게을러서가 아닐까?

Shawn 야, 내가 게으른 건 어떻게 알았냐? 너 직관력이 대단한데. 아무튼 내가 온라인 구매를 하는 또 다른 이유는 난 물건을 집으로 배송받는 게 좋더라고. 마치 선물을 받는 기분이 들어서.

Eve 그렇게 볼 수도 있겠네.

Sentence Building

prefer to + 동사 ~하는 게 더 좋다

I prefer to drink strong coffee than tea.
What would you prefer to do this weekend?

난 차 마시는 것보다 진한 커피를 더 좋아해.
이번 주말엔 무엇이 더 하고 싶니?

a little bit of both 두 가지 다 조금씩

Relax and read a book. I'll do a little bit of both this weekend.
Please do a little bit of both so we can get this done quicker.

쉬기도 하고 책도 읽고. 이번 주말엔 둘 다 조금씩 하려고.
두 가지 다 조금씩 해서 좀 더 빨리 끝내 보자.

Why didn't I think of that? 난 왜 그 생각을 못했을까?

That's such a great idea! Why didn't I think of that?
Why didn't I think of that? Then I'd get all the glory!

진짜 좋은 생각이야! 난 왜 그 생각을 못했을까?
난 왜 그 생각을 못 했지? 그랬으면 내가 모든 영광을 차지하는 건데!

intuitive 직관[직감]에 의한, 직관력이 있는

You're such an intuitive guy.
Gabby is so sexy and intuitive. It's like she knows all about me.

넌 직관력이 뛰어난 남자야.
개비는 섹시하기도 하고 직관력도 뛰어나. 마치 나에 대한 모든 것을 다 아는 것 같아.

Let's talk about today's topic.

1 What kinds of things do you buy from an online shop?

2 What is the benefit of buying something from an online shop?

3 Which retailer is your favorite and why?

Practice Questions

아래의 해석과 같은 의미가 되도록 빈칸을 채워 보세요.

1 Why don't you _____?
먼저 그걸 확인해 두는 게 어때?

2 Do you ever _____?
온라인 쇼핑을 해 본 적 있어?

3 I _____ drink strong coffee than tea.
난 차 마시는 것보다 진한 커피를 더 좋아해.

괄호 안의 어휘를 이용하여 영작해 보세요.

4 두 가지 다 조금씩 해서 좀 더 빨리 끝내 보자. (a little bit of both)

_____

5 난 왜 그 생각을 못 했지? 그랬으면 내가 모든 영광을 차지하는 건데!
(Why didn't I think of that?)

_____

6 넌 직관력이 뛰어난 남자야. (intuitive)

_____

Answers

❶ check it out first ❷ shop online ❸ prefer to ❹ Please do a little bit of both so we can get this done quicker. ❺ Why didn't I think of that? Then I'd get all the glory! ❻ You're such an intuitive guy.

Vocabulary Builder

빈칸에 들어갈 어휘를 상자 안에서 골라 적어 보세요.

> **prefer to**: preference for something else
>
> **shop online**: browse online retailers for stuff
>
> **check out**: look at
>
> **intuitive**: knowing something from your heart rather than thinking

1 I _____ eat sushi than cooked fish.

2 Hey, _____ the ad on TV! It has Suzy in it!

3 Let's _____ because we can get better deals that way.

4 He's so _____ and smart. I want to marry him some day.

Answers
❶ prefer to ❷ check out ❸ shop online ❹ intuitive

Buying directly from sites abroad

소리 내어 읽고 해석해 보세요.

Angie Oh, my God! Your TV is so huge! It must have **cost you a fortune**.

Bred **You would think, huh?** You know how much I got this for?

Angie I don't know, like, 5 million won?

Bred **Not even close. Try a little lower.**

Angie What? 4 million?

Bred 1.5 million won. **Isn't that something?**

Angie You **lucked out**! How was that even possible?

Bred I ordered it directly from Amazon when they had a big sale for Black Friday.

Angie You do that 'direct buying from abroad' thing? Isn't it kind of risky?

Bred Yes, it does have some risks involved, especially when you don't like the product, it's almost impossible to return it. However, when you think about the amount of money you can save, I think **it's worth the risk**.

Angie Hey, I want to try it too. Is it very **complicated**?

Bred Not at all. I can **show you how it's done**.

Vocabulary

cost someone a fortune 돈[비용]이 심하게 많이 들다
You would think, huh? 그렇게 생각하지? / 그럴 것 같지?
not even close 전혀 비슷하지도 않다
try lower 더 적은[낮은] 수치를 말해 봐
Isn't that something? 놀랍지? / 대단하지 않니?
luck out 운이 좋다
It's worth the risk. 위험을 감수할 만한 가치가 있다.
complicated 복잡한
show someone how it's done 어떻게 하는 것인지 보여 주다

해외 직구

Angie 우와! 너희 TV 엄청 크다! 진짜 비싸겠는데.

Bred 그렇게 보이지, 응? 이거 얼마 주고 샀게?

Angie 글쎄, 한 5백만 원?

Bred 완전히 틀렸어. 조금 더 낮춰 봐.

Angie 뭐야? 4백만 원?

Bred 백 오십만 원. 놀랍지 않니?

Angie 땡잡았네! 그게 도대체 어떻게 가능하지?

Bred 블랙프라이데이 빅 세일 할 때 아마존에서 바로 주문했지.

Angie 너 '해외 직구'라는 거 하는구나? 그거 좀 위험하지 않아?

Bred 응, 위험한 면도 없진 않아, 특히 제품이 마음에 안 들 땐 환불이 거의 불가능하거든. 그래도, 돈 아끼는 거 생각하면, 그 정도 위험은 감수해야지.

Angie 야, 나도 한번 해 볼래. 그거 하는 거 복잡해?

Bred 전혀. 어떻게 하는지 보여 줄게.

Sentence Building

cost someone a fortune 돈[비용]이 심하게 많이 들다

See this vase? It's from Japan. It costed me a fortune!
I don't want to get a new cellphone. It's going to cost me a fortune.

이 꽃병 보이지? 이게 일본에서 사 온 건데 엄청 비싼 거야!
새 휴대폰을 사고 싶지 않아. 거금이 들어갈 테니까.

You would think, huh? 그렇게 생각되지? / 그럴 것 같지?

You would think, huh? But there's no risk involved.
You would think I had a lot of money, huh? But I don't!

그럴 것 같지, 응? 하지만 위험 요소는 전혀 없어.
내가 돈이 정말 많을 것 같지, 응? 그런데 아냐!

luck out 운이 좋다

You really lucked out when you bought that last iPhone.
You weren't here to see the boss yell at everyone. You lucked out!

마지막으로 하나 남은 아이폰을 사다니 넌 정말 운이 좋구나.
사장님이 직원들한테 노발대발할 때 넌 없었구나. 참 운도 좋네!

show someone how it's done 어떻게 하는 것인지 보여 주다

You're such an amateur. Let me show you how it's done.
Can you show me how it's done?

넌 정말 아마추어구나. 어떻게 하는 건지 내가 보여 주지.
어떻게 해야 하는 건지 보여 줄 수 있니?

Let's talk about today's topic.

1. Have you ever purchased something abroad? What was it?

2. What are the risks/benefits of buying things from abroad?

3. What kinds of items are best bought outside your own country?

> **Practice Questions**

아래의 해석과 같은 의미가 되도록 빈칸을 채워 보세요.

1 That was _____.
전혀 비슷하지도 않았어.

2 It's more _____ than I thought.
생각보다 더 복잡하네.

3 I don't want to get a new cellphone. It's going to
_____.
새 휴대폰을 사고 싶지 않아. 거금이 들어갈 테니까.

괄호 안의 어휘를 이용하여 영작해 보세요.

4 그럴 것 같지, 응? 하지만 위험 요소는 전혀 없어.
(You would think, huh?)
_____

5 마지막으로 하나 남은 아이폰을 사다니 넌 정말 운이 좋구나. (luck out)
_____

6 어떻게 해야 하는 건지 보여 줄 수 있니? (show someone how it's done)
_____

Answers

❶ not even close ❷ complicated ❸ cost me a fortune ❹ You would think, huh? But there's no risk involved. ❺ You really lucked out when you bought that last iPhone. ❻ Can you show me how it's done?

Vocabulary Builder

빈칸에 들어갈 어휘를 상자 안에서 골라 적어 보세요.

> **try lower**: to choose a lower quantity
>
> **Isn't that something?**: That's amazing, right?
>
> **luck out**: to get lucky
>
> **complicated**: difficult to understand or deal with

1 Look at the baby walk. _____?

2 $400? No way. _____.

3 Learning this new software is so darn _____.

4 I want to _____ and get a job with a foreign company.

Answers
❶ Isn't that something? ❷ Try lower ❸ complicated ❹ luck out

Do you have religion?

소리 내어 읽고 해석해 보세요.

There's a saying that you should never talk about religion or **politics**. I totally agree with that. Talking about these subjects **creates conflict** among people. However, I want to talk about religion today. So, I'm going to go ahead and bring up the subject but not **in any controversial way**. I go to church and my girlfriend goes to a **Buddhist** temple, but we never **criticize** each other about that. We actually enjoy talking about the different culture and activities that we do there. It can be quite fun talking about the differences if you don't try to convince others to follow your religion. In fact, I wish I had more friends that **came from different religious backgrounds**.

Vocabulary

there's a saying ~라는 말[속담]이 있다
politics 정치
create conflict 갈등을 야기하다
in controversial way 논란이 되는 방식으로, 논란을 야기시키는 방식으로
Buddhist 불교신자
criticize 비난하다, 비판하다
come from different + 형용사 + backgrounds 자라 온[출신] 배경이 다른
religious background 종교적 배경

종교가 있나요?

흔히들 종교와 정치 얘기는 안 하는 게 좋다고 하지. 완전 동감. 그런 주제에 관해 얘기하면 갈등만 생기거든. 그렇지만, 난 오늘 종교 얘기를 하고 싶네. 종교 얘기를 하긴 하되 논란이 되지 않는 방식으로 해 보려고. 난 교회에 다니고 내 여자친구는 절에 다니지만 우린 서로의 종교에 대해서 절대 비판하지 않아. 오히려 그 두 종교의 문화 차이나 그 안에서 일어나는 일들에 관해서 이야기 나누는 것을 즐겨. 사실 서로의 종교를 믿으라고 설득하려 들지만 않는다면 그런 대화가 얼마나 재미있는데. 난 솔직히 다른 종교적 배경을 가진 친구들이 더 많았으면 좋겠어.

Sentence Building

there's a saying 이런 말[격언/속담]이 있다.

There's a saying, if you can't avoid it, enjoy it.
There's a saying, you get what you pay for.

이런 말이 있지, 피할 수 없다면 즐겨라.
이런 속담이 있어, 뿌린 만큼 거두는 법이다.

in a controversial way
논란이 되는 방식으로, 논란을 야기시키는 방식으로

I don't mean to bring up the subject in any controversial way.
Don't present it in a controversial way.

논란을 일으키려고 이 얘기를 꺼내는 건 아냐.
논란을 야기시키는 방식으로 발표하지 말아라.

criticize 비난하다, 비판하다

Stop criticizing yourself!
He always criticize everything I say.

스스로를 비난하지 좀 말아라!
그는 항상 내가 하는 말을 다 비판한다.

come from different + 형용사 + backgrounds
자라 온[출신] 배경이 다른

We just come from different economic backgrounds.
He comes from a different educational background.

우리가 사는[자라 온] 곳의 경제적 배경이 많이 다르네.
그는 교육적 배경이 다른 사람이야.

Let's talk about today's topic.

1 Are you religious? If you don't have one, what kind of religion do you want to have? If you do, what kind of religious activities do you do?

2 Are there any controversial subjects you don't talk about with your friends?

3 What is the best way to diffuse an awkward situation in a conversation?

Practice Questions

아래의 해석과 같은 의미가 되도록 빈칸을 채워 보세요.

1 Let's not talk about _____.
  정치 얘기는 하지 말자.

2 I'm a _____.
  난 불교신자야.

3 Don't present it _____.
  논란을 야기시키는 방식으로 발표하지 말아라.

괄호 안의 어휘를 이용하여 영작해 보세요.

4 이런 말이 있지, 피할 수 없다면 즐겨라. (there's a saying)
  _____

5 스스로를 비난하지 좀 말아라! (criticize)
  _____

6 그는 교육적 배경이 다른 사람이야.
  (come from a different + 형용사 + background)
  _____

Answers
❶ politics ❷ Buddhist ❸ in a controversial way ❹ There's a saying, if you can't avoid it, enjoy it. ❺ Stop criticizing yourself! ❻ He comes from a different educational background.

Vocabulary Builder

빈칸에 들어갈 어휘를 상자 안에서 골라 적어 보세요.

> **there's a saying**: a common phrase or idiom usually follows this
>
> **controversial**: something people don't want to talk about
>
> **criticize**: to judge something
>
> **religious background**: a person's religious upbringing

1 Don't _____ the movie if you haven't even seen it yet.

2 Talking about sexuality is so _____ in our society.

3 What's Luke's _____? Did he grow up Catholic or what?

4 _____, the bigger they are the harder they fall.

Answers
❶ criticize ❷ controversial ❸ religious background ❹ There's a saying

Podcasts

소리 내어 읽고 해석해 보세요.

Noah (**Giggles**) This is so funny.

Sally What are you doing **talking to yourself**?

Noah I'm listening to this podcast. These guys are **hilarious**.

Sally Podcast? What is that?

Noah Oh, don't you know? It's an internet radio show.

Sally An internet radio show? **How is that any different from** regular or traditional radio shows?

Noah Oh, man, this is a thousand times better because the regular radio shows have so many **restrictions** where these don't. And since anybody can make podcast programs and **put them up online,** lots of crazy fun ideas and subjects can be discussed.

Sally Wow! That sounds exciting. Would you recommend some programs?

Noah Surely. Let me just show you the ones that I **subscribe to**.

Sally Subscribe? Does that mean you have to pay for these?

Noah Absolutely not. They are all **free of charge**!

Vocabulary

giggle 킥킥거리다, 히죽히죽 웃다
talk to oneself 혼잣말하다, 혼자서 중얼거리다
hilarious 아주 웃긴, 신나는
How is that any different from ~? ~하고 뭐가 달라? / ~와 다를 게 뭐가 있어?
restriction 제약, 제한
put something up online 인터넷상에 게재하다
subscribe to ~을 구독하다
free of charge 공짜, 무료

팟캐스트

Noah   (키득거리며) 이거 진짜 웃긴다.

Sally   너 왜 혼잣말하고 앉아 있냐?

Noah   팟캐스트 듣고 있었어. 이 사람들 진짜 웃겨.

Sally   팟캐스트? 그게 뭔데?

Noah   아, 몰라? 인터넷에서 하는 라디오 방송이야.

Sally   인터넷 라디오 쇼? 그거하고 일반 라디오 방송하고 뭐가 다른데?

Noah   거 참, 이게 천 배는 더 좋아, 왜냐하면 보통 라디오 방송에는 제약이 너무 많은데 이건 안 그렇거든. 그리고 누구나 팟캐스트 프로그램을 만들어서 온라인에 올릴 수 있기 때문에, 수많은 기발한 아이디어와 주제를 논할 수 있어.

Sally   와! 진짜 재밌겠다. 프로그램 좀 추천해 줄래?

Noah   그래. 내가 구독하는 거 보여 줄게.

Sally   구독? 돈을 내야 한단 말이야?

Noah   절대 그럴 리 없지. 다 공짜야!

Sentence Building

talk to oneself 혼잣말하다, 혼자서 중얼거리다

Sometimes I notice old ladies on the subway talking to themselves.
I like talking to myself when I try to solve a problem.

가끔 보면 어떤 할머니들이 지하철에서 혼잣말로 떠들고 있더라.
난 혼자 중얼거리면서 문제 푸는 게 좋더라.

How is that any different from ~?
~하고 뭐가 달라? / ~와 다를 게 뭐가 있어?

How is that any different from what I suggested earlier?
How is that any different from what already exists?

내가 아까 제안했던 것하고 뭐가 달라?
그게 이미 있는 것하고 다를 게 뭐가 있어?

subscribe to ~을 구독하다

I subscribe to a number of YouTube channels.
Do you subscribe to the newspaper?

난 유튜브 채널들을 여러 개 구독하고 있어.
신문 구독하니?

free of charge 공짜, 무료

When you buy this book, you get a notebook free of charge.
Is this candy here free of charge?

이 책을 사면, 공책을 공짜로 받을 수 있어.
여기 이 사탕 공짜예요?

Let's talk about today's topic.

1 Do you listen to any podcasts? Which ones?

2 How will entertainment change in the next ten years?

3 What is the best way of getting information?

Practice Questions

아래의 해석과 같은 의미가 되도록 빈칸을 채워 보세요.

1 What are you _____ about?
그 뭐 때문에 그렇게 킥킥거리고 있니?

2 The movie was _____.
그 영화 정말 웃기더라.

3 I like _____ when I try to solve a problem.
난 혼자 중얼거리면서 문제 푸는 게 좋더라.

괄호 안의 어휘를 이용하여 영작해 보세요.

4 내가 아까 제안했던 것하고 뭐가 달라?
(How is that any different from~?)

_____

5 신문 구독하니? (subscribe to)

_____

6 여기 이 사탕 공짜예요? (free of charge)

_____

Answers

❶ giggling ❷ hilarious ❸ talking to myself ❹ How is that any different from what I suggested earlier? ❺ Do you subscribe to the newspaper? ❻ Is this candy here free of charge?

Vocabulary Builder

빈칸에 들어갈 어휘를 상자 안에서 골라 적어 보세요.

> **giggle**: to laugh in a silly way
>
> **hilarious**: something really funny
>
> **restriction**: a limit on something
>
> **subscribe**: you join to receive more
>
> **free of charge**: no cost

1 This new comedy show is so _____.

2 I _____ to many different podcasts with different genres.

3 Is there a _____ on how many bottles of alcohol I can buy?

4 When you buy a pack of four, you get a fifth one _____.

5 I _____ when I see people falling down in videos.

Answers
❶ hilarious ❷ subscribe ❸ restriction ❹ free of charge ❺ giggle

Unit 28 Fitness craze

소리 내어 읽고 해석해 보세요.

Having six-pack abs is on my **bucket list**. Why don't I just try getting them now? I wish I could, but it really is a lot harder than it sounds. **To tell you the truth**, I have tried a couple times but it just didn't work. Yes, I admit that I'm a **quitter**, but you would know just how difficult it is if you **tried it yourself**. But is it really worth it? I mean, what's all this **fuss about** fitness? Do we really need to spend so much time and energy only to impress others? I know, being in shape and having a **perfect figure** would make you feel great about yourself, but **too much is too much**. How about we try to spend just a little more time on more **meaningful** things like, I don't know, maybe reading or helping others or spending time with family?

Vocabulary

bucket list 죽기 전에 해야 할 것들 목록
six-pack abs 식스팩 복근 *abs = abdominal muscles
to tell you the truth 실은, 솔직히 말하자면
quitter 중도 포기자
try something oneself 직접 해 보다, (신발이나 옷, 안경 등을) 직접 신어[입어] 보다
fuss about ~에 대한 야단법석[소란/난리]
perfect figure 완벽한 몸매
too much is too much 이미 허용치를 넘어서다, 그만 좀 하자
meaningful 의미 있는, 중요한

몸짱 열풍

식스팩 복근 만드는 게 내 버킷 리스트 중 하나야. 지금 하면 되지 않느냐고? 나도 물론 그러고 싶지, 그런데 이게 생각보다 진짜 어려워. 실은, 전에 몇 번 시도해 봤는데 실패했거든. 그래, 내가 끈기가 없다는 것은 인정, 하지만 너도 도전해 보면 그게 얼마나 힘든지 알 걸. 근데, 식스팩 복근 만드는 게 정말 가치 있는 일이기나 한 걸까? 내 말은, 다들 몸짱 한번 돼 보겠다고 왜 이렇게 난리들인 거지? 단지 남들 보기 좋으라고 이렇게 공을 들여야 하는 거야? 물론 건강도 챙기고 몸매도 좋아지면 완전 기분 좋겠지만, 요즘 세태를 보면 좀 과한 것 같아. 몸짱이 되려고 애쓰기보다 좀 더 의미 있는 일에 말하자면, 나도 잘은 모르지만, 책을 읽는다거나, 다른 사람들을 돕거나, 가족과 시간을 보내는 것에 좀 더 시간을 쓰면 어떨까?

Sentence Building

to tell you the truth 솔직히 말하자면

To tell you the truth, I don't think those shoes look good.
To tell you the truth, I can't really play baseball well.

솔직히 말하자면, 그 신발 이상해.
솔직히 말하자면, 나 야구 잘 못해.

try something oneself
직접 해 보다, (신발이나 옷, 안경 등을) 직접 신어[입어] 보다

You can't criticize it unless you try it yourself.
Try it for yourself and see if you like it.

네가 직접 해 보기 전까지는 비판하면 안 되는 거야.
직접 입어 보시고 맘에 드는지 한번 보세요.

fuss about ~에 대한 야단법석[소란/난리]

What's all the fuss about these honey butter chips?
Do you know what all the fuss is about?

허니버터 칩에 대해 왜 그리 소란인 거야?
뭐 때문에 이리 야단법석인지 아니?

too much is too much 이미 허용치를 넘어서다, 그만 좀 하자

I love chocolate, but too much is too much.
It's fun to do, but too much is too much.

초콜릿이 정말 좋긴 하지만, 너무 많이 먹은 것 같아.
재밌긴 한데, 이제 그만 좀 하지.

Let's talk about today's topic.

1 What do you think about the fitness or hot-body craze?

2 Do you have any wishes about your body type or health?

3 How can one stay as healthy as possible?

Practice Questions

아래의 해석과 같은 의미가 되도록 빈칸을 채워 보세요.

1 Amy has a _____.
에이미는 몸매가 완벽해.

2 Do something _____ with your life.
내 인생에 있어서 의미 있는 일을 해라.

3 _____, I can't really play baseball well.
솔직히 말하자면, 나 야구 잘 못해.

괄호 안의 어휘를 이용하여 영작해 보세요.

4 네가 직접 해 보기 전까지는 비판하면 안 되는 거야.
(try something oneself)
_____

5 뭐 때문에 이리 야단법석인지 아니? (fuss about)
_____

6 재미있긴 한데, 이제 그만 좀 하지. (too much is too much)
_____

Answers

❶ perfect figure ❷ meaningful ❸ to tell you the truth ❹ You can't criticize it unless you try it yourself. ❺ Do you know what all the fuss is about? ❻ It's fun to do, but too much is too much.

Vocabulary Builder

빈칸에 들어갈 어휘를 상자 안에서 골라 적어 보세요.

> **six-pack abs**: abs that look like the top of a six-pack of beer
>
> **bucket list**: things you want to do before you die
>
> **quitter**: somebody who quits things a lot
>
> **fuss**: popular talk, worry or get excited about something unimportant
>
> **meaningful**: full of significance or purpose

1 Skydiving is on my _____.

2 I think I'd look really hot with _____.

3 When I receive praise from my boss, it's so _____ to me.

4 I'm not a _____. I'll keep going until I succeed!

5 What's all the _____ about this new drama on TV?

Answers
❶ bucket list ❷ six-pack abs ❸ meaningful ❹ quitter ❺ fuss

Tattoos

소리 내어 읽고 해석해 보세요.

Getting a tattoo is **in fashion**. When I watch TV, I see so many celebrities with tattoos, especially those professional baseball and basketball players. You may call me old-fashioned, but the **instant image** that **pops into my head** when I think of tattoos is **heinous** gangsters with large dragons or snakes on their backs. I still feel a little scared when I see someone with a tattoo. I heard it is pretty expensive to get a nice tattoo, **not to mention** the pain you have to **go through** when you get one. And **what's worse**, getting it removed hurts even more. I'm sure there are a lot of people out there that get them for fashion and think they're cool and beautiful. But if you ask me, it's going to take a long time for me to **get used to** it.

Vocabulary

in fashion 유행하는
instant image 즉각 떠오르는 이미지
pop into one's head 머릿속에 불현듯 떠오르다, 바로 생각이 떠오르다
heinous 악랄한, 극악무도한
not to mention ~는 말할 것도 없고, ~는 물론이고
go through ~을 겪다, 거치다, 검토하다
what's worse 더 심한 건, 그보다 더 짜증나는 건
get used to ~에 익숙해지다

문신

문신하는 게 유행이다. TV에서 보면, 문신을 한 유명인들이 참 많은데, 특히 그중에서도 프로 야구선수들과 농구선수들이 눈에 띈다. 나더러 구식이라고 말할지 모르겠지만, 문신 하면 내 머릿속에 바로 떠오르는 이미지는 등에 큰 용이나 뱀 문신을 한 살벌한 깡패들이다. 지금도 문신한 사람들을 보면 좀 겁이 난다. 제대로 된 문신 하나 하려면 엄청 아픈 건 말할 것도 없고 돈도 많이 든다는데. 게다가 나중에 문신을 지우려고 하면 훨씬 더 아프다던데. 점점 많은 사람이 문신을 멋지고 아름다운 패션의 일종이라고 생각하는 것 같다. 그런데 개인적인 생각으로는, 난 아무래도 이런 문화에 익숙해지려면 시간이 꽤 오래 걸릴 것 같네.

Sentence Building

pops into one's head
머릿속에 불현듯 떠오르다, 바로 생각이 떠오르다

What's the first thing that pops into your head when I say "beautiful"?
The first thing that pops into my head is usually the right answer.

'아름답다'라고 하면 가장 먼저 머릿속에 떠오르는 게 뭐니?
맨 처음에 머릿속에 떠오른 게 정답일 가능성이 높더라고.

not to mention ~은 말할 것도 없고, ~는 물론이고

It's delicious, not to mention healthy too.
It's really affordable, not to mention easy to get.

건강에 좋다는 건 말할 것도 없고, 맛있기까지 해.
구하기 쉬울 뿐만 아니라, 값도 싸.

what's worse 더 심한 건, 그보다 더 짜증나는 건

What's worse, you have to wait two weeks for it to arrive.
What's worse, I've got to do twice as much work while he's gone.

더 짜증나는 건, 2주나 기다려야 받을 수 있다는 거야.
더 심한 건, 그가 없는 동안 일을 두 배나 더 해야 한다는 거야.

get used to ~에 익숙해지다

I can never get used to the fact that I'm getting older.
Oh, you lost? Well, get used to it! I'm going to win again!

내가 늙어 가고 있다는 사실에 난 절대 익숙해지질 않아.
아, 네가 졌다고? 에이, 익숙해져! 내가 또 이길 거거든!

Let's talk about today's topic.

1 What are you opinions on tattoos?

2 Why have tattoos gotten so popular in recent years?

3 If you got a tattoo, what would you get and where?

Practice Questions

아래의 해석과 같은 의미가 되도록 빈칸을 채워 보세요.

1 Blue is _____ this year.
올해는 파란색이 유행이야.

2 The guy committed a _____ crime.
그 남자는 극악무도한 범죄를 저질렀어.

3 The first thing that _____ is usually the right answer.
맨 처음에 머릿속에 떠오르는 것이 정답일 가능성이 높더라고.

괄호 안의 어휘를 이용하여 영작해 보세요.

4 건강에 좋다는 건 말할 것도 없고, 맛있기까지 해. (not to mention)

_____

5 더 짜증나는 건, 2주나 기다려야 받을 수 있다는 거야. (what's worse)

_____

6 내가 늙어 가고 있다는 사실에 난 절대 익숙해지지 않아. (get used to)

_____

Answers

❶ in fashion ❷ heinous ❸ pops into my head ❹ It's delicious, not to mention healthy too.
❺ What's worse, you have to wait two weeks for it to arrive. ❻ I can never get used to the fact that I'm getting older.

Vocabulary Builder

빈칸에 들어갈 어휘를 상자 안에서 골라 적어 보세요.

> **in fashion**: many people want to buy it
>
> **pop into one's head**: suddenly comes to mind
>
> **heinous**: very terrible
>
> **not to mention**: also, in addition to, as well as
>
> **get used to**: to become accustomed to

1 I can't _____ eating with a fork and knife every day.

2 The murder we saw on TV is such a _____ crime!

3 Her phone number just _____. Write this down.

4 It's really amazing, _____ cheap.

5 Big lacey boots are so _____ right now.

Answers
❶ get used to ❷ heinous ❸ popped into my head ❹ not to mention ❺ in fashion

Fortune-telling

소리 내어 읽고 해석해 보세요.

Nate   Have you ever been to a **psychic**?

Erin   What kind of a psychic are you talking about? Are you **referring to** 'jum', the traditional Korean fortune telling or tarot card reading or **palm reading** or **face reading**? Which one? 'Cause I've been to almost all of them.

Nate   Are you serious? Do you believe in that **supernatural** stuff?

Erin   Not really. **It's just that** my mom loves going to those places and she takes me with her whenever she goes to one of them.

Nate   Wow, that's really interesting. Tell me more about it! Are they pretty accurate?

Erin   Some of them are better than others. But mostly I think they just **make stuff up as they go along**. You know like saying stuff that generally applies to anyone really.

Nate   Like what?

Erin   Like 'you must be concerned about your daughter not getting married, aren't you?'

Nate   Haha. That's so **obvious**.

Vocabulary

psychic 점쟁이, 심령술사, 초능력자
refer to ~에 대해 언급하다[얘기하다], ~을 참조하다
palm reading 손금 보기
face reading 관상 보기
supernatural 초자연적인
It's just that (+ 주어 + 동사) 그냥 ~해서 그래
make something up as someone goes along
이야기를 진행하면서 말을 지어내다
obvious 누가 봐도 뻔한, 명백한

점

Nate 너 점 본 적 있어?

Erin 어떤 종류의 점? (점쟁이가 보는) 한국 전통 '점', 아니면 타로점, 손금, 관상? 어떤 거? 난 웬만한 데는 거의 다 가 봤거든.

Nate 진짜야? 그런 미신을 믿는단 말이야?

Erin 아니 별로. 그냥 우리 엄마가 그런 곳에 가는 걸 좋아해서 갈 때마다 날 데리고 가시거든.

Nate 와, 흥미진진한데. 좀 더 얘기해 봐! 점이 잘 맞긴 해?

Erin 어떤 사람들은 꽤 잘하더라고. 그런데 대부분 그냥 우리 얘기 듣고 말을 지어내는 것 같아. 귀에 걸면 귀걸이 코에 걸면 코걸이 같은 얘기들 있잖아.

Nate 예를 들면 어떤 거?

Erin 그러니까 뭐 '당신 딸이 결혼하지 않아 걱정하고 있구먼, 안 그래?' 이런 거.

Nate 하하. 진짜 너무 뻔하네.

Sentence Building

refer to ~에 대해 언급하다[얘기하다], ~을 참조하다

Let me refer to the manual to see if I can get a better answer.
Are you referring to the mole on my face when you say I'm ugly?

그것에 대한 더 적절한 답이 있을지에 대해서는 매뉴얼을 참조하도록 하자.
나보고 못생겼다고 하는 게 내 얼굴에 있는 사마귀를 두고 하는 말이니?

It's just that + 주어 + 동사 그냥 ~해서 그래

It's just that I don't like you like I used to.
It's just that I don't know where this relationship is going.

그냥 내가 널 예전처럼 좋아하지 않아서 그래.
우리 관계가 아무래도 더는 의미가 없는 것 같아서 그래.

make something up as someone goes along
이야기를 진행하면서 말을 지어내다

Why are you making this up as you go along?
I don't know what to do. I'll just make it up as I go along.

왜 얘기를 하는 도중에 말을 지어내고 그러니?
어떻게 해야 좋을지 모르겠어. 그냥 진행하면서 할 이야기를 지어낼게.

obvious 누가 봐도 뻔한, 명백한

It's obvious you really like Kelly.
It's so obvious that he doesn't know what he's doing.

네가 켈리를 많이 좋아한다는 것은 누가 봐도 다 알 정도야.
그는 자기가 뭘 하고 있는지 모른다는 게 너무도 명백해.

Let's talk about today's topic.

1. Have you ever been to a fortune teller or psychic?

2. If you could know your future, would you want to know it?

3. Do you believe in supernatural things?

Practice Questions

아래의 해석과 같은 의미가 되도록 빈칸을 채워 보세요.

1. A _____ is a person who is sensitive to energy.
   심령술사는 기에 대해서 예민한 사람이다.

2. Julie has _____ powers.
   줄리는 초자연적인 힘을 가지고 있어.

3. Are you _____ the mole on my face when you say I'm ugly?
   나보고 못생겼다고 하는 게 내 얼굴에 있는 사마귀를 두고 하는 말이니?

괄호 안의 어휘를 이용하여 영작해 보세요.

4. 그냥 내가 널 예전처럼 좋아하지 않아서 그래.
   (It's just that + 주어 + 동사)

   _____

5. 왜 얘기를 하는 도중에 말을 지어내고 그러니?
   (make something up as someone goes along)

   _____

6. 네가 켈리를 많이 좋아한다는 것은 누가 봐도 다 알 정도야. (obvious)

   _____

Answers
❶ psychic ❷ supernatural ❸ referring to ❹ It's just that I don't like you like I used to.
❺ Why are you making this up as you go along? ❻ It's obvious you really like Kelly.

Vocabulary Builder

빈칸에 들어갈 어휘를 상자 안에서 골라 적어 보세요.

> **psychic**: someone who can perceive the future
>
> **refer to**: use something else as a point of information
>
> **supernatural**: not of the real world
>
> **accurate**: exact
>
> **obvious**: well-known

1. Ghosts are _____ beings that haunt houses, right?

2. Let me _____ this guide on how to use this particular phone.

3. Isn't it _____ that we're lost? There's nothing around!

4. The weather report is never totally _____.

5. I need to see a _____ before I apply for the job.

Answers
❶ supernatural ❷ refer to ❸ obvious ❹ accurate ❺ psychic

영어회화 3단계 집중 훈련

팟캐스트
영어
스터디

초판 1쇄 인쇄   2016년 04월 15일
초판 1쇄 발행   2016년 04월 20일

지은이   라이언 강
발행인   홍성은
발행처   바이링구얼
교정·교열   임나윤
디자인   이초희
출판등록   2011년 01월 12일
주 소   서울 양천구 신정로 275, 202-601
전 화   (02) 6015-8835
팩 스   (02) 6455-8835
메 일   nick0413@gmail.com

ISBN   979-11-85980-14-0 13740

• 잘못된 책은 구입한 서점에서 바꿔 드립니다.